Survivors

High-Interest Nonfiction

by
Brenda Holt McGee
and
Debbie Triska Keiser

Carson-Dellosa Publishing Company, Inc.
Greensboro, North Carolina

Dedicated to my grandmother, Margie Leonard;
a true survivor who taught me to be one.
—Brenda McGee

Credits

Editor: Wolfgang Hoelscher

Layout Design: Mark Conrad

Inside Illustrations: Allana Kereluk

Cover Design: Peggy Jackson

Cover Illustrations: Tara Tavonatti

ISBN 0-88724-950-7

Table of Contents

Introduction

Invite your students to experience the thrill of reading with the exciting stories in *Survivors: High-Interest Nonfiction*.

The passages in this book are appropriate for students in the intermediate grades. Among these grade levels, and even within individual classrooms, you will find learners at all different reading levels. When presenting students with a new text, there is always the danger of either frustrating struggling readers or boring those students who have jumped ahead. To help all of these students maintain interest and find success in their reading assignments, this book presents each passage written at two reading levels.

Also included with each passage is a set of comprehension questions that applies to both versions and a bonus activity. The questions test students' skills in determining main idea, reading for details, sequencing, using context clues, and drawing conclusions. The bonus activity is a writing extension that reinforces reasoning skills and encourages students to connect prior knowledge with the text.

An assessment grid at the back of the book makes it easy to see which reading comprehension skills each student has mastered.

An icon in the lower right or left corner of each passage designates the reading level.

A 🔦 indicates the higher-level version.

A 🧭 indicates the lower-level version.

Use the rubric below to help you assess your students' writing after they have completed the bonus writing extension following each passage.

	Novice 1	Emerging 2	Independent 3	Distinguished 4	N/A
Topic	Did not stay on topic	Stayed on topic for most of the paragraph	Stayed on topic	Stayed on topic with elaboration	
Organization	Not organized	Organized	Well organized	Outstanding organization	
Written Expression	Hard to understand	Could understand most	Easy to understand	Well written, elaborated	

4

Buried Alive

Have you ever played in the snow? It's soft, cold, and wet. As it falls, it brushes against your cheeks and feels like butterfly wings touching your face. But if too much snow falls in the mountains it can be dangerous. Winston Cheyney learned this the hard way. He was buried alive in an avalanche!

Winston and two friends were mountain climbing in Colorado. His friend Jeff was leading the way up the mountain with Winston in the middle and his other friend Gene behind them. Jeff was making footprints in a snow bank. Winston was supposed to step in the same places as Jeff. As he was walking, Cheyney remembers that his feet broke through the footprint into really soft snow.

Suddenly, the snow bank they were on made a loud cracking noise. Jeff was at the top of the bank and Gene was at the bottom. They quickly moved out of the way. Winston, though, was right in the middle and knew he was caught in an avalanche.

Being a trained mountain climber, he remembered what to do. He made swimming motions with his arms and legs to help him stay on top of the snow. Then, he was thrown into the air and landed by a large rock. As the snow began to bury him, he remembered to put his arms near his face to create an air space. Soon he couldn't move because the weight of the snow had made him **immobile**.

After being buried, Winston began to panic and soon became unconscious. Thirty minutes later, his friends found him and dug him out. Winston knows he survived because he created the air space under the snow. It pays to be prepared!

Buried Alive

Snow is soft, cold, and wet. As it falls, it feels like butterfly wings touching your face. But if too much snow falls in the mountains it can be risky. Winston Cheyney learned this the hard way. He was buried alive in an avalanche!

Winston and two friends were mountain climbing in Colorado. His friend Jeff led the way up the mountain. Jeff was making footprints into a snow bank. Winston was supposed to step in the same places as Jeff. As Cheyney was walking, his feet broke through the footprint into really soft snow.

Suddenly, the snow bank made a loud noise. Jeff was at the top of the bank and their other friend Gene was at the bottom. They quickly moved out of the way. But Winston was right in the middle. He was caught in an avalanche.

Being a trained mountain climber, he knew what to do. He made swimming motions with his arms and legs. This helped him stay on top of the snow. Then, he was thrown into the air and landed by a large rock. The snow began to bury him. He put his arms near his face to create a space for air. Then, he couldn't move. The weight of the snow made him **immobile**.

After being buried, Winston began to panic. Soon he fainted. Thirty minutes later, his friends found him and dug him out. Winston knows he survived because he created the air space under the snow. It pays to be prepared!

Buried Alive

1. What was the main idea of the first paragraph?
   A. Even though snow is soft and fun, it can be dangerous.
   B. Playing in the snow is fun.
   C. Avalanches are dangerous.
   D. Winston Cheyney was in an avalanche.

2. Answer the following questions.

   Where were the men hiking when the avalanche occurred?

   _____

   Why did Winston start "swimming" in the snow?

   _____

   Where was Jeff during the avalanche?

   _____

   How long did it take his friends to dig him out?

   _____

3. Number the following events in the order they happened.

   _____ Jeff and Gene dug Winston out of the snow.
   _____ Winston made swimming motions with his arms and legs.
   _____ Jeff led the way, making steps up the mountain for the others.
   _____ Winston, Jeff, and Gene went hiking in the Colorado mountains.
   _____ They heard a loud noise.

4. What does the word **immobile** mean in the story?
   A. faint
   B. sick
   C. unable to breathe
   D. unable to move

5. Why do you think Winston survived?
   A. The snow wasn't as packed as he thought it was.
   B. The avalanche he was in wasn't that bad.
   C. He didn't panic at first and he remembered what to do when caught in an avalanche.
   D. He was able to dig himself out quickly.

Bonus:
Write a paragraph telling how an avalanche and a flood are alike and different.

7

Enduring Antarctica

Imagine a help-wanted sign that reads: "Men needed for a dangerous trip. Little pay and brutal cold. Will spend months in total darkness. Little chance of a safe return." In 1914, Sir Ernest Shackleton, a famous British explorer, posted an advertisement like this and waited to see if anyone would sign up. He wanted to be the first to lead an expedition across the frozen continent of Antarctica at the bottom of the world.

Amazingly, twenty-seven men accepted Shackleton's challenge. Seeking nothing but adventure, they told him they would go with him.

Shackleton had been to Antarctica twice before and was anxious to return. He and his crew set sail from London on a wooden ship called *Endurance*. They were only a day away from land when their ship got stuck in a sea of floating ice. They were trapped with no other humans around for thousands of miles. No one would come to rescue them.

For ten months, they lived on the boat. In Antarctica, the sun doesn't shine in the winter. It was cold, dark, and lonely.

Then, things got much worse. The ice started to crush the *Endurance*, turning its wooden sides into splinters. The men had to abandon ship in a hurry and watch it sink. Now they were forced to live outside on the ice. There was no way to get home except for the three small lifeboats they managed to save.

The crew drifted on ice for five months. Finally, land was sighted, and the crew sailed the boats to the shore. But the island they'd discovered was **uninhabitable**. They had to move on if they were going to be rescued.

Shackleton took five men and one lifeboat in hopes of finding another island named South Georgia. There were people on this island who could save them. The only problem was that the trip was 800 miles long through some of the harshest waters in the world.

Seventeen days later, they landed on South Georgia. They hiked across the island, climbing snowy mountains, to reach the only town. Shackleton borrowed another ship and rescued the rest of his men. Somehow, all twenty-eight men made it home safely. Everyone survived!

Enduring Antarctica

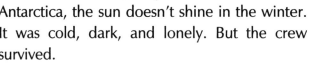

Sir Ernest Shackleton was a famous British explorer. He had been to Antarctica twice. In 1914, he wanted to go back. This time, he wanted to be the first to cross the frozen continent at the bottom of the world.

He and his crew of twenty-seven men sailed from London to Antarctica on a wooden ship called *Endurance*. They were a day away from land when their ship got stuck in a sea of floating ice. They were trapped. There were no other humans around for thousands of miles. No one would come to save them.

For ten months, they lived on the boat. In Antarctica, the sun doesn't shine in the winter. It was cold, dark, and lonely. But the crew survived.

Then, things got worse. The ice started to crush the *Endurance*. The men had to leave the ship. They watched it sink. Now they had to live outside on the ice. There was no way to get home except for the three small lifeboats they managed to save.

The crew drifted on ice for five months. Finally, the men made it to land. Still, the island they found was **uninhabitable**. They had to move on if they were going to be rescued.

Shackleton took five men and one lifeboat to find an island named South Georgia. There were people on this island who could save them. The only problem was that the trip was 800 miles long. There were strong winds and bitter cold.

Seventeen days later, they landed on South Georgia. They hiked across the island, climbing snowy mountains, to reach the only town. Shackleton found another ship and rescued the rest of his men. Somehow, all twenty-eight men made it home safely. Everyone survived!

CD-4320 Survivors: High-Interest Nonfiction

Name: _____

1. Choose the best title for this story.
   A. Floating Ice
   B. Crossing Antarctica
   C. A Trip to South Georgia
   D. Stranded at the Bottom of the World

2. Answer the following questions.

   When doesn't the sun shine in Antarctica?

   _____

   How long did the men drift on the ice after their ship sank?

   _____

   When Shackleton landed on the shore of South Georgia, what did he have to do next?

   _____

   How many lifeboats did the crew save?

   _____

3. Number the following events in the order they happened.

   _____ Shackleton rescued his crew.

   _____ The *Endurance* was stuck in the ice.

   _____ Shackleton took a lifeboat to South Georgia Island.
   _____ The crew abandoned ship.

   _____ The crew lived on floating ice after their ship sank.

4. What does the word **uninhabitable** mean in the story?
   A. unbelievable
   B. unlivable
   C. unusual
   D. unsteady

5. What conclusion can you make about Ernest Shackleton's character?
   A. He was reckless.
   B. He liked boats.
   C. He always dreamed of finding the North Pole.
   D. He wasn't afraid of danger.

Bonus:

Shackleton's crew was told that the trip would be dangerous with little pay. Why, then, do you think twenty-seven men signed up for this trip? Write a paragraph to explain your answer.

Everybody's Baby

For a moment in time, an 18-month-old baby belonged to the world. The country watched as volunteers tried to save a little Texas girl.

Jessica McClure fell 22 feet into a well. Her mother had set her down in her sister's backyard while she answered the phone. A minute later, Baby Jessica tumbled into the eight-inch-wide hole.

Jessica cried as rescue workers first tried to save her. But they couldn't do it alone. They needed help. Jessica appeared to be stuck in the pipe. They had to be careful because one wrong move and she could fall hundreds of feet.

Within hours the crowd watching grew to over fifty people. **Experts** were called in to help. Mining and drilling engineers, police officers, and support people arrived. They came up with a plan and flew in special equipment from around the world. Everyone worked together as a team.

They pumped air into the well to keep Jessica alive. Then, a tunnel was dug beside the well. The first step was to make sure she couldn't fall any farther. Next, they would tunnel over to her and bring her out.

It seemed as though the world stopped as people crowded around television sets to cheer for the men and women helping in the rescue.

It was a very dramatic moment when Jessica was finally lifted out. Baby Jessica had been in the well for a little over 58 hours.

This event happened in 1987. Today, Jessica is a happy and healthy young lady. She says that she is proud of the few scars she has because they remind her that she is a true survivor.

 CD-4320 Survivors: High-Interest Nonfiction

Everybody's Baby

Jessica McClure was only 18-months old when she fell 22 feet into a well. Her mother had set her down in her sister's backyard while she answered the phone. A minute later, Baby Jessica fell into the eight-inch-wide hole.

Rescue workers first tried to save the little Texas girl. But they couldn't do it alone. They needed help. They also had to be careful. Jessica seemed to be stuck in the pipe. With one wrong move, she could fall hundreds of feet.

Soon, a large crowd grew. **Experts** in mining and drilling were brought in to help. Police officers and firefighters arrived, too. They flew in special tools from around the world. Everyone worked together as a team.

They pumped air into the well to keep Jessica alive. Then, a tunnel was dug beside the well. The first step was to make sure she couldn't fall farther. Next, they would tunnel over to her and bring her out.

People crowded around television sets to cheer for the rescuers. When they finally lifted Jessica out of the well, it was a very exciting moment. Baby Jessica had been in the well for over 58 hours.

This event happened in 1987. Today, Jessica is a happy and healthy young lady. She says that she is proud of the few scars she has. She says they remind her that she is a survivor.

Everybody's Baby

1. What is the main idea of the passage?
   A. Jessica was in her backyard.
   B. Jessica had scars from falling into a well.
   C. Rescuers worked hard to save a baby trapped in a well.
   D. People watched the rescue on television.

2. Answer the following questions.

   How old was Jessica when she fell into the well?

   _____

   Where did Jessica and her mother live?

   _____

   When did this happen?

   _____

   How many hours was Jessica in the well?

   _____

3. Number the following events in the order they happened.

   _____ Jessica fell into the well.

   _____ Air was pumped into the well to help Jessica breathe.
   _____ Jessica was pulled out of the well.

   _____ Jessica's mother left to answer the phone.
   _____ Experts were called in to help.

4. In the story, what does the word **experts** mean?
   A. people who build mines
   B. people who dig wells
   C. people who know a lot about a subject
   D. people who give first aid to those with injuries

5. Why do you think so many people cared about a baby they didn't know?
   A. Most people have wells in their backyards.
   B. People were worried about Jessica's safety.
   C. People knew Jessica's mother and wanted to help her.
   D. People were interested in moving to Texas.

Bonus:
Imagine that you were Jessica's next-door neighbor when she fell into the well. Write about what you saw from your bedroom window.

First American in Space

Space travel is taken for granted today. Unless there is something unusual about the mission or the crew, space flights rarely make the news. There was a time when that was very different.

Before the 1960s, people only dreamed about space travel. Movies were made about it. Books and comics were written about it, too. Nobody believed space flight could happen. They didn't think a human could survive the force it would take to blast a rocket into space. Even if it were possible, the chances of surviving in space and returning home safely seemed impossible.

Alan Shepard was a test pilot for the United States Navy. He helped change America's view of space travel. In 1959, he was among seven men chosen to train as astronauts. On May 5, 1961, he was strapped into a rocket and blasted

off into space. The first American-manned space flight lasted just 15 minutes. Shepard was sent 116 miles straight up and then returned to Earth, landing safely.

Shepard returned to space in 1971. He was in charge of the Apollo 14 mission to the moon. Shepard was the fifth person to walk on the moon but the first to play golf on the **lunar** surface.

After his historic space flight and walk on the moon, he continued to serve his country in the U.S. Navy. He retired in 1974. Shepard received many honors and medals during his life. He wrote a book about his many travels in space before his death in 1998.

First American in Space

Americans take space travel for granted today. It doesn't seem unusual. Space flights hardly ever make the news. But there was a time when that was very different.

Before the 1960s, people only dreamed about space travel. Movies were made about it. People wrote books and comics about it, too. But no one thought humans could travel into space. How could a person survive taking off in a rocket? Even if they could, how would they get home?

Alan Shepard was a test pilot for the United States Navy. His bravery helped change America's view of space travel. In 1959, NASA chose him to train as an astronaut. He was one of only seven men picked for the job. Then, on May 5, 1961, he was strapped into a rocket and blasted off into space. The first American-manned space flight lasted just 15 minutes. The rocket took Shepard 116 miles straight up. Then, he returned to Earth and landed safely.

Shepard went back into space in 1971. He led a mission to the moon. Shepard was the fifth person to walk on it. However, he was the first to play golf on the **lunar** surface.

Shepard retired in 1974. He received many honors and medals. Then, he wrote a book about his many space travels. Shepard died in 1998.

CD-4320 Survivors: High-Interest Nonfiction

First American in Space

1. What is the main idea of the third paragraph?
   A. The first space flight lasted 15 minutes.
   B. Shepard went up 116 miles into space.
   C. Shepard became the first American in space.
   D. Shepard strapped himself into a rocket.

2. Answer the following questions.

   When was Shepard's first space flight?

   _____

   When did Shepard retire?

   _____

   How many men were chosen to be astronauts in 1959?

   _____

   What unusual thing did Shepard do when he walked on the moon?

   _____

3. Number the following events in the order they happened.

   _____ Shepard was chosen for astronaut training.
   _____ Shepard walked on the moon.

   _____ Shepard was strapped into a rocket in 1961.
   _____ Shepard retired.

   _____ Shepard was a test pilot.

4. What does the word **lunar** mean in the story?
   A. belonging to the moon
   B. lime
   C. rough
   D. smooth

5. Why do think Shepard was chosen to be an astronaut?
   A. Shepard liked danger.
   B. Shepard was a good test pilot.
   C. Shepard dreamed of going to the moon.
   D. Shepard could fit easily in the rocket.

Bonus:

The very first man in space was a Russian named Yuri Gagarin. He beat Shepard into space by one month. Write a paragraph about how you think Shepard felt when he learned that he wouldn't be the first man in space.

Sacagawea

The United States has a gold dollar coin. On one side of it is a picture of a young Native-American girl with her baby. Her name was Sacagawea, and she was a true survivor.

In 1800, an enemy tribe kidnapped Sacagawea. She was only about twelve years old. They took her hundreds of miles away from her Shoshone home. They made her a slave. Later, she was married off to a fur trader who was twice her age.

Four years later, Sacagawea had a chance to make history. With her husband by her side and her newborn son strapped to her back, she joined a group of explorers. Meriwether Lewis and William Clark would lead this group across the American Northwest to find a way to the Pacific Ocean. She was the only woman in the group of over thirty men.

Sacagawea helped the men find plants to eat when they were hungry. She also acted as their **interpreter** when they met Native Americans. She helped them talk to the different tribes they met. At one point, the explorers came across a group of Shoshones. She soon realized that the chief of the tribe was her brother. It had been more than five years since she had seen him. After she was welcomed back by her people, the explorers were helped. They got the food, guides, and the horses they needed.

Without her help, the journey may not have been a success. At one point, while canoeing down a river, Sacagawea jumped into the water. She saved the explorers' journals that had fallen overboard. Lewis and Clark kept these journals to record the events of the journey. If she hadn't acted bravely then, we may not have learned as much about the explorers' adventures.

The explorers safely returned home from their long trip, thanks to the help of Sacagawea. The next time you see a gold dollar, you will know why that brave, young Native-American girl was honored.

Sacagawea

The United States has a gold dollar coin. On one side of it is a picture of a young Native-American girl with her baby. Her name was Sacagawea. She was a survivor.

In 1800, an enemy tribe captured Sacagawea. She was only about twelve years old. They took her hundreds of miles away from her Shoshone home. They made her a slave. Later, she was married off to a fur trader who was twice her age.

Four years later, Sacagawea joined a group of explorers. Meriwether Lewis and William Clark wanted to find a way to the Pacific Ocean. They would lead the group across the American Northwest. Sacagawea went with her husband. Her baby son was strapped to her back. She was the only woman in the group of over thirty men.

Sacagawea found plants for the men to eat. She was also their **interpreter** when they met Native Americans. She helped them talk to the different tribes. Once, the explorers came across a group of Shoshones. She quickly saw that the chief was her brother. She had not seen him in five years. Her people welcomed her back. Soon, the explorers were helped. They got the food, guides, and horses they needed.

Without her help, the trip may not have been a success. At one point, she saved the explorers' journals. They had fallen out of a canoe into a river. Sacagawea jumped into the water to get them. These journals told about the trip. If she hadn't saved them, we may not have learned as much about Lewis and Clark.

The explorers returned home safely. They made it thanks to the help of Sacagawea. Now you know why that brave Native-American girl is on the dollar coin.

Sacagawea

1. What is the main idea of the fourth paragraph?
   A. Sacagawea helped the explorers survive.
   B. The explorers made discoveries during the exploration.
   C. The life of a Shoshone woman was hard.
   D. Sacagawea saw the Pacific Ocean.

2. Answer the following questions.

   About how old was Sacagawea when an enemy tribe captured her?

   _____

   What area were Lewis and Clark hoping to explore?

   _____

   What is the value of the coin that Sacagawea is on?

   _____

   Into what Native-American tribe was Sacagawea born?

   _____

3. Number the following events in the order they happened.
   _____ Sacagawea found her brother whom she hadn't seen in five years.
   _____ Sacagawea was kidnapped.

   _____ Sacagawea joined the Lewis and Clark Expedition.
   _____ Sacagawea got food, guides, and horses for the expedition.
   _____ Sacagawea was married.

4. What does the word **interpreter** mean in the story?
   A. someone who offers a gift of food
   B. someone who makes a trade
   C. someone who asks questions
   D. someone who helps two groups who don't speak the same language understand each other

5. Why do you think Lewis and Clark wanted to bring Sacagawea with them on their trip?
   A. They thought she was nice.
   B. They needed her help to talk to the Native Americans they met.
   C. They knew she was a good swimmer.
   D. They wanted to save her from her kidnappers.

Bonus:
On the trip with Lewis and Clark, Sacagawea saw the ocean for the first time in her life. Write a paragraph about what you think this might have been like for her.

Setting a Record

Do you know how to protect yourself against lightning? Roy C. Sullivan could have helped you answer that question. He learned the hard way. You could even say his story is a little shocking.

Roy was hit by lightning seven times in 35 years. That is a world **record**. Each year, about one thousand people are struck by lightning and about one hundred of those people die. Even those that survive can have brain damage or other serious injuries. After being struck seven times, Roy lost a toenail and both eyebrows. Lightning once set his hair on fire. He also had scars on his shoulder, chest, stomach, ankle, and leg.

Roy became a serious weather watcher and knew all about lightning. He certainly knew that you can't outrun it. A bolt of lightning can travel over 60,000 miles per second. Lightning can even run underground, traveling many feet from where it touched down.

There are some steps you can take to protect yourself from lightning. First, pay close attention to weather reports before going outside. As soon as you see lightning or hear thunder, seek shelter in a nearby building. If you're not close to a building, get in a car, if possible. If neither of these are options for you, then move away from tall objects, such as trees or flagpoles, that lightning is more likely to strike. Avoid open fields or water. You should sit down or lay flat on the ground. This way you won't be the tallest object in the area. That may feel silly, but it could prevent injuries or even death.

Roy Sullivan never set out to be a record holder. He knew that being struck by lightning is serious business. He was a very lucky man.

Setting a Record

Roy C. Sullivan was hit by lightning seven times. That is a world **record**. Each year, about one thousand people are struck by lightning. About one hundred of those people die. Lightning can also cause some bad injuries. Roy lost a toenail and both eyebrows. His hair was once set on fire. He also had scars on his shoulder, chest, stomach, ankle, and leg.

Roy became a serious weather watcher. He knew all about lightning. He knew that you can't outrun it. A bolt of lightning can travel over 60,000 miles per second. Lightning can even run underground. It can travel many feet from where it touched down.

There are some steps you can take to protect yourself from lightning. First, pay attention to weather reports before going outside. As soon as you see lightning or hear thunder, find a nearby building. If you're not close to a building, get in a car, if possible. If you can't do either, then move away from tall things that lightning is more likely to strike, such as trees or flagpoles. Stay away from open fields or water. You should sit down or lay flat on the ground. This way you won't be the tallest thing in the area. That may feel silly, but it could save your life.

Roy Sullivan never wanted to set a record. He knew that being hit by lightning is bad news. He was a very lucky man.

Setting a Record

Name: _____

1. Choose another title for this passage.
   A. Dangerous Trees
   B. Weather Watching
   C. Beware of Lightning
   D. Seeking Shelter

2. Answer the following questions.

   Where should you go at the first sign of lightning?

   _____

   About how many people are struck by lightning every year?

   _____

   How fast can lightning travel?

   _____

   How many times was Roy Sullivan struck by lightning?

   _____

3. When lightning strikes, you should try to do the following in order:

   _____ Get away from tall objects like trees and flagpoles.
   _____ Lie flat on the ground.

   _____ Seek shelter from the storm in a building.
   _____ Seek shelter from the storm in a car.

   _____ Learn to watch weather reports.

4. What does the word **record** mean in this passage?
   A. a vinyl disc used to play music
   B. a newspaper story
   C. an action recognized by everyone
   D. an event

5. What conclusion can you make about lightning from this passage?
   A. It never strikes the same place twice.
   B. It's beautiful to watch.
   C. It only strikes metal objects.
   D. It's dangerous and should be avoided.

Bonus:

Imagine you are interviewing Roy C. Sullivan for a newspaper story. What would you ask him?

22

CD-4320 Survivors: High-Interest Nonfiction

Surviving Septuplets!

Most people have children one at a time. Bobbi and Kenny McCaughey of Iowa have had quite a different family experience.

The McCaugheys already had one daughter. Then, they found out they were expecting another child. Soon they got some exciting news. They weren't just having one baby. They were having seven! Seven babies from the same mother at the same time are called "septuplets."

On November 19, 1997, Bobbi had four tiny boys and three tiny girls. The babies were born premature. They had to stay in the hospital a while before going home.

The septuplets were very popular children. They were in the news around the world.

The family received many gifts. A lifetime supply of diapers was given to the babies. This was a huge gift. The children would use at least 75,000 diapers before being potty trained. Baby formula, clothing, and a large van were **donated**, too. People in their community built a large house for the family.

How did the parents survive feeding seven hungry babies each night? People from their town offered their time. Volunteers came to their house around the clock to help feed the babies. The babies also needed diaper changes, baths, and rocking. The helpers didn't let the McCaugheys down. They spent over 70,000 hours helping with the babies.

The McCaughey family survives each day because everyone works together. And together they will raise their large, precious family.

23

Surviving Septuplets!

Most people have children one at a time. Bobbi and Kenny McCaughey of Iowa did it differently.

The McCaugheys already had a daughter. Then, they found out they were going to have another child. Soon they got some exciting news. They weren't just having one baby. They were having seven! Seven babies from the same mother at the same time are called "septuplets."

On November 19, 1997, they had four boys and three girls. The babies were born early. They were tiny, too. They couldn't go home at first. They had to stay in the hospital.

The septuplets were very popular children. They were in the news around the world.

The family got many gifts. One was a lifetime supply of diapers. This was a big gift. The children would use at least 75,000 diapers before being potty trained. Baby formula, clothing, and a large van were **donated** to them, too. People in their town even built a large house for the family.

How did the parents survive each day? People from their town helped them. Volunteers cared for the babies all day long. They fed, bathed, and rocked them. They changed their diapers. They washed clothes and cut the grass. The helpers didn't let the McCaugheys down. Over 70,000 hours were spent helping with the babies.

The McCaughey family survives each day by working together. And together they will raise their large, special family.

Surviving Septuplets!

1. What was the main idea of the second to last paragraph?
   A. People helped the McCaughey family.
   B. The children needed to be fed.
   C. The parents were tired after caring for the kids all day.
   D. The babies needed to be bathed.

2. Answer the following questions.

   How many children did the McCaugheys have altogether?

   _____

   How many hours were donated to helping the McCaughey family in total?

   _____

   On what date were the babies born?

   _____

   What was built for the family?

   _____

3. Number the following events in the order they happened.

   _____ The McCaugheys had septuplets.

   _____ The McCaugheys had a daughter.

   _____ The babies got a lifetime supply of diapers.
   _____ Volunteers came to help with the babies.
   _____ The McCaugheys found out they were having septuplets.

4. What does the word **donated** mean in the story?
   A. bought
   B. taken
   C. had
   D. given

5. Why do you think so many people gave time and money to help the McCaugheys?
   A. They wanted to be in the news for helping the family.
   B. People knew it would be hard to raise seven babies and wanted to help.
   C. People wanted to spend time with Bobbi and Kenny.
   D. People wanted to be paid money for helping the family.

Bonus:
Write a paragraph telling if you would like to have seven brothers and sisters who were the same age.

25

Think Tall

They said he'd never make it. They laughed when he wanted to play. But Spud Webb proved them wrong. At just five feet, seven inches tall, he did more than just survive in a world of giants. He became a superstar.

Webb says he has a gift. He has the ability to jump. That makes up for his height when he plays basketball with men at least a foot taller than him. At one time he was reported to have a 50-inch **vertical** jump. Even with so much talent, he had a tough time breaking into a sport dominated by tall men.

Even though Webb scored more than 30 points in each of his high school games, colleges just weren't interested. They saw his lack of height as a problem. Finally, one coach took a

chance. Webb was offered a basketball scholarship to a small college in Midland, Texas. Webb got noticed when that college won their championship with Webb as point guard. After that, North Carolina State University offered Webb a chance to play for them. The bigger school meant more opportunities.

Even with all of the national attention Webb got in college, the National Basketball Association (NBA) was still hesitant to sign him as a professional player. Only one team was interested. The Atlanta Hawks gave him a try. The rest is history. Webb started his first year as a professional winning the Slam-Dunk Contest at the NBA All-Star Game. He amazed everyone. He also set many other records before retiring after a twelve-year career.

Webb says he always knew he wanted to play professional basketball, but it took years of hard work and practice. Most importantly, he never stopped believing in himself.

Think Tall

They said he'd never make it. They laughed when he wanted to play. But Spud Webb proved them wrong. At just five feet, seven inches tall, he did more than just survive in a world of giants. He became a superstar.

Webb plays basketball with men at least a foot taller than him. But, he has a gift. He can jump very high. That makes up for his height. At one time, people said he had a 50-inch **vertical** jump. However, he still had a tough time. Breaking into a sport played only by tall men was not easy.

In each of his high school games, Webb scored more than an amazing 30 points. But, colleges still weren't interested. They saw his height as a problem. Finally, one coach took a chance. Webb was asked to play for a small college in Midland, Texas. Webb got noticed when that college won their championship. After that, North Carolina State offered Webb a chance. He played for them, too.

However, professional teams were still not sure about Webb. Only one team was interested in him. The Atlanta Hawks gave him a try. The rest is history. Webb started his first year as a professional winning the All-Star Slam Dunk Contest. Basketball fans will never forget this. He also set many other records. After twelve years, Webb finally retired.

Webb says he always knew he wanted to play professional basketball. It took years of hard work and practice. Most importantly, he never stopped believing in himself.

CD-4320 Survivors: High-Interest Nonfiction

Think Tall

1. What is the main idea of this story?
   A. Spud Webb is a short man.
   B. Spud Webb is a great jumper.
   C. Spud Webb worked hard for something he wanted.
   D. Spud Webb played for twelve years.

2. Answer the following questions.

   How high do some people believe Webb can jump?

   _____

   For what professional team did Spud Webb play first?

   _____

   How tall is Spud Webb?

   _____

   About how many points did Webb score for his high school team in every game?

   _____

3. Number the following events in the order they happened.

   _____ Webb won the All-Star Slam Dunk contest.
   _____ Webb retired from basketball.

   _____ Webb played for North Carolina State.
   _____ Webb realized he had a gift.

   _____ Webb played for a college in Midland, Texas.

4. What does the word **vertical** mean in the story?
   A. up and down
   B. front and back
   C. left and right
   D. backward and forward

5. Why do you think it was so hard for Webb to break into professional basketball?
   A. Webb wasn't a very good basketball player in high school.
   B. People had a hard time believing a short man could play professional basketball.
   C. Webb was shy and didn't fight to be heard.
   D. Short men weren't allowed to play professional basketball.

Bonus:

Imagine you are Spud Webb and have been asked to give a talk to a class. What would you say? Write about what you would want people to learn from your experience in basketball.

Tornado!

The weather reports were **ominous** by afternoon, and people were alarmed. One day in 1999, the worst tornado in Oklahoma history was about to strike.

Paden Conley and his family lived in Oklahoma City. The day began as any other. Paden went to work while his wife, Sherrie, was at home with their children, Gant and Lake. The weather forecast was getting worse by five o'clock that afternoon. Sherrie called Paden and asked him to come home.

When Paden arrived, he found his family safely hiding in a hallway closet. It was windy and raining, and soon it began to hail. Paden went to the porch to collect some hailstones. He didn't think the tornado was really going to hit. But then Paden looked up and saw that the sky was as black as night. He couldn't see the tornado. Suddenly, cars and mailboxes on his street were flying into the air. He knew then that the tornado was coming.

He hurried inside and scrambled into the closet. He held the baby, Gant, between his legs, put his arm through Lake's shirt, and grabbed hold of Sherrie. Then, the tornado hit.

It was deafening. It sounded like a locomotive. First, they heard things striking the house. Then, all the windows shattered. The house started shaking, and suddenly, the roof blew off. It sounded like an explosion. Paden and his family were pelted with hail, rain, and other debris as the tornado blew away their house.

As suddenly as it began, the storm was over, and there was only silence. Paden and his family dug their way out of the rubble. All that was left of their house was the closet in which they had hidden. They knew they were fortunate to have survived the tornado. That day, they learned that nothing else matters as long as you have your family.

Tornado!

Weather reports were **ominous**. People were scared. One day in 1999, the worst tornado in Oklahoma history was about to strike.

Paden Conley and his family lived in Oklahoma City. The day began as any other. Paden went to work. Sherrie, his wife, was home with the children. Weather forecasts were worse by five o'clock that afternoon. Sherrie called Paden. She asked him to come home.

When Paden got home, it was windy and raining. His family was safely hiding in a closet. It began to hail. Paden went to the porch to get hailstones. He didn't think the tornado was going to hit. He couldn't see it. Then, he saw cars and mailboxes flying into the air. The tornado was coming!

He ran inside and climbed into the closet. He put the baby between his legs. Then, Paden put his arm through his other son's shirt and held Sherrie. Suddenly, the tornado hit.

It sounded like a train. First, they heard things hitting the house. Then, all the windows broke. The house started to shake. Suddenly, the roof blew off. It sounded like an explosion. Paden and his family were hit with hail, rain, and other things as the tornado roared. It blew their house away.

As suddenly as it began, the storm was over. There was silence. Paden and his family dug their way out. All that was left of their house was the closet in which they had hidden. They knew they were lucky to survive the tornado. They learned that nothing else matters as long as you have your family.

Tornado!

1. What was the main idea of the fourth paragraph?
   A. Paden ran inside.
   B. The tornado was coming.
   C. Paden held his family as the tornado hit.
   D. Paden held his son's shirt.

2. Answer the following questions.

   Where did this tornado strike?

   _____

   In what year did the tornado strike?

   _____

   Where were Paden and his family during the tornado?

   _____

   What did the tornado sound like?

   _____

3. Number the following events in the order they happened.

   _____ Paden picked up hailstones.

   _____ They heard things hitting the house.

   _____ The roof came off the house.

   _____ Paden climbed into the closet with his family.

   _____ The windows broke in the house.

4. What does the word **ominous** mean in the story?
   A. boring
   B. calming
   C. threatening
   D. funny

5. Why do you think Paden and his family were lucky?
   A. They were lucky because the tornado probably didn't hurt their car.
   B. They were lucky because they survived the worst tornado in Oklahoma history.
   C. They were lucky because Paden got hailstones before the tornado.
   D. They were lucky because Sherrie was home.

Bonus:

Suppose you knew that a tornado was on its way, and you could pick one thing to save from the storm. Write a paragraph about what that thing would be and why you would choose it.

Be Safe, Not Sorry

Eighteen-year-old Adam Taliaferro was doing what he did best, playing football. He was only a freshman at Penn State University when he got his big chance. With two minutes left in the game, he was called out onto the field.

Adam says he remembers running onto the field and getting hit. Everything turned dark after that. The next thing he remembers is waking up on the field with doctors and trainers standing over him. He also recalls that he attempted to get up but his body wouldn't respond.

A hush fell over the crowd. Was Adam paralyzed? If Adam had injured his spinal cord, chances were there wouldn't be a happy ending. Each year, about 10,000 Americans are **partially** or completely paralyzed by spinal cord injuries. Most are young men.

Adam was very fortunate. Penn State's team doctor knew that it was important not to move him. His neck and body were strapped to a board so he couldn't move. In the ambulance, they gave him medicine to prevent swelling.

When Adam got to the hospital, he was examined. The doctors discovered that his spinal cord was bruised, not severed. That was good news, but not great news. The doctors told Adam's father he only had a 1 in 10 chance of ever walking again.

Adam never knew that the odds were against him. He slowly began to get feeling back in his legs. His limbs were exercised for him until he could do it himself. Four months later, Adam walked out of the hospital on crutches. Today, he walks just fine. He wants to go back to playing football, but he won't. He survived one spinal cord injury. That's enough for anyone.

Be Safe, Not Sorry

Eighteen-year-old Adam Taliaferro loved playing football. He had just started at Penn State University when he got his big chance. With two minutes left in the game, he was called out onto the field.

Adam says he remembers running onto the field. Then, he got hit. Everything went dark. Doctors were standing over him when he woke up. He couldn't move his body.

The crowd was quiet. They wondered if Adam would walk again. Had he hurt his spinal cord? Each year, about 10,000 Americans are **partially** or completely crippled by spinal cord injuries. Most are young men.

Adam was very lucky. Penn State's team doctor knew what to do. It was important not to move him. His neck and body were strapped to a board so he couldn't move. He was then given medicine to help stop swelling.

When Adam got to the hospital, the doctors saw that his spinal cord was bruised. It wasn't broken. That was good news, but not great news. The doctors told Adam's father he only had a 1 in 10 chance of ever walking again.

Adam never knew that the odds were against him. He slowly began to get some feeling back in his legs. Four months later, Adam walked out of the hospital on crutches. Today, he walks just fine. He wants to go back to playing football, but he won't. He survived one spinal cord injury. That's enough for anyone.

CD-4320 Survivors: High-Interest Nonfiction

Be Safe, Not Sorry

Name: _____

1. This story tells about:
   A. how to prevent spinal cord injuries.
   B. a famous football player.
   C. the way one athlete survived a spinal cord injury.
   D. a mystery.

2. Answer the following questions.

   How old was Adam Taliaferro when he was injured?

   _____

   What is the most important thing to remember when you think someone has a spinal cord injury?

   _____

   For what school did Adam play football?

   _____

   About how many people are partially or completely paralyzed each year?

   _____

3. Number the following events in the order they happened.

   _____ Adam started to get feeling back in his legs.
   _____ Adam was strapped to a board to keep him from moving.
   _____ Adam walked out of the hospital on crutches.
   _____ Adam ran onto the football field.
   _____ Adam was hit.

4. What does the word **partially** mean in this story?
   A. somewhat
   B. totally
   C. permanently
   D. temporarily

5. What conclusions can you draw about the team doctor?
   A. He loves football and other sports.
   B. He wants to work in a hospital.
   C. He knows how to handle injuries.
   D. He has a big family.

Bonus:

Imagine you were a sports reporter covering the football game. Write a news story about what happened to Adam.

Flesh-Eating Bacteria

Vance "Bo" Salisbury is a survivor of flesh-eating bacteria. Few people get this **disease**, and many don't survive it. Bo was playing soccer with some of his friends when he was kicked in the ankle. The injury didn't bother him until the next day. Then, the pain got so unbearable that his wife took him to the emergency room at the local hospital.

The doctors couldn't make a diagnosis, so they sent him home. The next day the pain was more than he could tolerate. He was also sick to his stomach and unable to walk. His doctor put him in the hospital and started running tests.

The next morning, Bo's vital organs started shutting down. He needed help breathing. Finally, the doctors were able to diagnose what was wrong. Bo had been exposed to flesh-eating bacteria. They would have to start him on a powerful medicine and remove the infected skin. That meant taking off his skin down to his muscle. As the disease spread, the same surgical process was done five more times. At that point, the doctors thought it would be impossible for Bo to recover. But suddenly the disease stopped spreading. The doctors said it was a miracle.

To make sure all of the bacteria was gone, much of his skin was removed. Healthy skin was taken from the rest of his body and put on the open wounds. The long healing process began.

Today, Bo's leg won't win any beauty contests, but he can walk fine. He's back at work and glad to be a survivor.

35

Flesh-Eating Bacteria

Vance "Bo" Salisbury was sick because of something called flesh-eating bacteria. Few people get this **disease**. Many don't survive it.

While playing soccer one day, Bo was kicked in the ankle. The injury didn't bother him until the next day. Then, the pain got so bad, his wife took him to the hospital.

The doctors couldn't figure out what was wrong with him. So they sent him home. The next day, he couldn't stand the pain. He was also sick to his stomach and unable to walk. His doctor sent him to the hospital again and started running tests.

The next morning, Bo was worse. He needed help breathing. Finally, the doctors were able to tell what was wrong. Bo had flesh-eating bacteria. They would have to put him on a strong medicine. The infected skin would

have to be removed down to the muscle. As the disease spread, the doctors took off more skin. They didn't think Bo would live. But suddenly, the disease stopped spreading. The doctors said it was a miracle.

To make sure all of the bacteria was gone, much of Bo's skin was removed. Healthy skin was taken from the rest of his body and put on the open wounds. The long healing process began.

Today, Bo's leg isn't pretty, but he can walk fine. He's back at work and glad to be a survivor.

Flesh-Eating Bacteria

1. Choose another title for the story.
   A. Life in a Hospital
   B. A Strange Disease
   C. Soccer Injuries
   D. Going Home

2. Answer the following questions.

   What part of Bo's body did he injure while playing soccer?

   _____

   What disease did Bo have?

   _____

   Why did they keep removing skin?

   _____

   With what did they cover the open wounds?

   _____

3. Number the following events in the order they happened.

   _____ Bo went back to work.

   _____ Bo went to the hospital but was sent home.

   _____ Bo was kicked while playing soccer.

   _____ Skin was removed from most of his body.

   _____ The doctors started running tests.

4. What does the word **disease** mean in the story?
   A. problem
   B. situation
   C. emergency
   D. illness

5. What can you tell about flesh-eating bacteria after reading about Bo's experience?
   A. Only men can get the disease.
   B. It's difficult for doctors to diagnose the disease.
   C. It's best to wait before going to the hospital if you think you have it.
   D. You can only get the disease if you play soccer.

Bonus:
Write a paragraph about how you would feel if this happened to a friend or family member. What would you say to that person, and what would you do to try and help?

Presidential Survivor

F ranklin D. Roosevelt was one of the most popular United States presidents. He was the only president to be elected to four terms. He was special in many ways.

First, he did great things for the country. When he became president in 1933, the United States was in terrible shape. More people were out of work than ever before. Roosevelt came up with ideas that got people back to work. He made sure **legislation** was passed that set up rules to protect the poor, elderly, and disabled. He also led the country to victory during World War II.

Second, Roosevelt was special because he survived a terrible illness. When he was 39 years old, Roosevelt was diagnosed with polio. It is a disease that damages your muscles. Most often it affects the legs, but it can involve any muscles, including those that control breathing and swallowing. It left Roosevelt without the use of his legs.

In Roosevelt's time, disabled people were expected to stay out of sight. People didn't respect them. Roosevelt worried that when he ran for president, people would not vote for him. He thought people would see his disability as a weakness. He hid it when he could. He never let anybody photograph him being carried. He also wore his leg braces under his clothes. It worked. Roosevelt was elected.

There is still no cure for polio, but now it is easy to prevent. There is a vaccine that babies get to keep them from getting this disease. This same vaccine is being used around the world. Roosevelt, a man of the people, would be happy to know about this improvement.

Presidential Survivor

eople liked Franklin D. Roosevelt. That's why they elected him to four terms as president. He was special in many ways.

First, he did great things for the United States. When he became president in 1933, the country was in bad shape. Many people were out of work. He came up with ideas to get people jobs. He made sure **legislation** was passed. It set up rules to protect the poor, elderly, and disabled. He also led the country to win World War II.

Roosevelt was also special because he survived a bad illness. When he was 39 years old, Roosevelt was told he had polio. It is a sickness that harms your muscles. It left Roosevelt without the use of his legs.

In Roosevelt's time, disabled people weren't respected. Roosevelt worried that people would not vote for him. He thought people would see his disability as a weakness.

So he hid it when he could. He never let anyone take a picture of him being carried. He also wore his leg braces under his clothes. It worked. Roosevelt was elected.

There is still no cure for polio. However, there is a way to prevent people from getting it now. Roosevelt would be happy to know this.

39

Presidential Survivor

Name: _____

1. What was the main idea of the third paragraph?
   A. Roosevelt had polio.
   B. Roosevelt was elected four times.
   C. Roosevelt lost the use of his legs.
   D. Polio affects your muscles.

2. Answer the following questions.

   When did Roosevelt get polio?

   _____

   Where did Roosevelt wear his leg braces?

   _____

   Roosevelt was President during which war?

   _____

   If a term is four years, how many years could Roosevelt have been President?

   _____

3. Number the following events in the order they happened.

   _____ Roosevelt became President.

   _____ Roosevelt was told he had polio.

   _____ Roosevelt protected the poor, elderly, and disabled.
   _____ Doctors can stop people from getting polio now.
   _____ Roosevelt ran for President.

4. What does the word **legislation** mean in the story?
   A. taxes
   B. paperwork
   C. laws
   D. funding

5. Why do you think it was so important to Roosevelt to protect the disabled?
   A. He thought people with disabilities couldn't do anything for themselves.
   B. He thought people would like him more.
   C. He just thought it was a good idea.
   D. He understood how it felt to be disabled.

Bonus:

Should Roosevelt have hidden his disability when he was running for president? Write what you think about this.

Umpire to the Rescue

What do you do if you're eating at a restaurant and suddenly hear someone getting mugged right outside? If you are Steve Palermo, professional baseball umpire, you run to the rescue.

It was a summer night in Dallas, Texas, 1991. Steve was having dinner with friends at an Italian restaurant. He had just finished umpiring a game. He was about to fly home to Kansas City when his life changed forever.

Steve, along with six other men, bolted out the front door to help the two women in trouble. They grabbed one of the muggers. The other two drove away. Steve and a friend pinned the man to the ground. They were waiting for police when they heard squealing tires and the sound of gunfire. The two muggers were coming back and shooting at them.

A bullet cut through Steve's kidney and into his spinal cord. He was paralyzed instantly. At the hospital, the doctors weren't sure they could save him. But they did. Steve would live, but the doctors said he probably would never walk again.

Steve would not accept this. He worked hard in physical therapy. To almost everyone's surprise, four months after the shooting Steve walked from a dugout to throw out the first pitch of a World Series game.

Today, Steve walks with a limp and uses a cane. He serves as one of Major League Baseball's four umpire supervisors. He says he misses the excitement of **officiating** a game, but he doesn't regret what he did. He has been a true inspiration to so many who have suffered from paralysis.

CD-4320 Survivors: High-Interest Nonfiction

Umpire to the Rescue

What would do you do if you heard someone getting mugged nearby? If you are Steve Palermo, professional baseball umpire, you run to the rescue.

It was a summer night in Dallas, Texas. Steve had just finished umpiring a game. He was having dinner with friends at an Italian restaurant when his life changed forever.

Steve and six other men ran out the front door. They helped the two women in trouble. They grabbed one of the muggers. The other two drove away. Steve and a friend pulled the man to the ground. They were waiting for police when they heard squealing tires and the sound of gunfire. The two muggers were coming back and shooting at them.

A bullet cut through Steve's kidney and into his spinal cord. At the hospital, the doctors weren't sure they could save him. But they did. Steve would live, but the doctors said he probably would never walk again.

Steve wouldn't give up. He worked hard to get better. Four months after the shooting, he surprised everyone. At a World Series game, Steve walked from a dugout to throw out the first pitch.

Today, Steve walks with a limp and uses a cane. He now supervises other umpires. He says he misses the thrill of **officiating** a game. But Steve doesn't feel sorry about what he did. Now many people, both in and out of sports, look up to him.

Umpire to the Rescue

1. What is the main idea of the third paragraph?
   A. Two women were being mugged.
   B. Steve and six others rescued two women from muggers.
   C. Steve grabbed one of the muggers.
   D. The muggers shot at Steve.

2. Answer the following questions.

   How many muggers were there?

   _____

   Where was Steve shot?

   _____

   What was Steve's new job?

   _____

   Where did Steve throw out the first pitch?

   _____

3. Number the following events in the order they happened.

   _____ Steve was taken to the hospital.

   _____ Steve umpired a baseball game in Dallas, Texas.

   _____ Steve was eating dinner when the muggers attacked.

   _____ Steve walked out of a dugout four months after the shooting.

   _____ Steve and a friend pulled one of the muggers to the ground.

4. What does the word **officiating** mean in the story?
   A. watching
   B. playing
   C. rating
   D. judging

5. Why do you think people look up to Steve?
   A. He had worked in baseball for many years.
   B. He was a great umpire.
   C. He was brave and tough.
   D. He was in the World Series.

Bonus:

Has anyone ever told you that you wouldn't be able to do something, but you proved them wrong? Write about a time this happened to you.

Stranded in Antarctica!

r. Jerri Nielsen was looking for a change. She had worked in an emergency room for many years. She wanted to do something different. Then, she found a job that would take her to the bottom of the world. She could be a doctor in Antarctica!

After passing several physical exams, it was decided that Jerri could go. There is one problem with going to Antarctica for the winter. You have to stay for eight and a half months until it warms up enough for an airplane to come get you.

Jerri was prepared to stay for an exciting year in Antarctica. She would be the only doctor for the Antarctic station for eight months. She left the United States for Antarctica in the fall of 1998. But by early March of the next year, Jerri knew she had a problem.

She had found a lump in her breast. She thought it might be cancer. When the tumor didn't go away after three months, she told her co-workers and family about it.

A cancer doctor contacted Jerri in June. The high-tech tests he gave her showed that Jerri definitely had cancer. Special planes flew over the station and dropped supplies needed for treating cancer. Her friends at the station helped her with her **treatments**.

At first, the tumor shrank. Then, it began to grow again. Jerri's cancer doctor said she needed to get back to the United States. She needed treatment in a hospital as soon as possible.

In October 1999, an airplane landed at the station for three minutes to pick up Jerri and drop off the new doctor. Jerri was soon back home. She had more treatments and then surgery. The surgery was a success. Jerri is a survivor of cancer. She also survived one of Earth's harshest climates.

44

Stranded in Antarctica!

r. Jerri Nielson was looking for a change. She had worked in an emergency room for many years. She wanted to do something different. Then, she found a job that would take her to the bottom of the world. She could be a doctor in Antarctica!

Jerri passed several physical exams. She could go to Antarctica. There was one problem with going there for the winter. She had to stay for eight months. Airplanes can't fly to Antarctica in the winter.

Jerri was ready to go. She would be the only doctor at the station. She left home in the fall of 1998. But by early March of the next year, Jerri knew she had a problem.

She had found a lump in her breast. She thought it might be cancer. The lump didn't go away. She told her friends and family about it.

A cancer doctor helped Jerri. The tests he gave her showed that Jerri definitely had cancer. Special planes flew over the station. They dropped some supplies. These supplies were for treating cancer.

Her friends at the station helped give her medicine. At first, the lump got smaller. Then, it grew again. Jerri needed to get back home. She needed treatment as soon as possible.

In October, an airplane landed at the station. It was there for three minutes. A new doctor arrived to replace Jerri. The plane took Jerri back home. She had **treatments** and surgery. Jerri is a survivor of cancer. She also survived one of Earth's harshest climates.

CD-4320 Survivors: High-Interest Nonfiction

Stranded in Antarctica!

1. What is the main idea of the first paragraph?
   A. Dr. Jerri Nielson needed a change.
   B. Dr. Jerri Nielson needed a vacation.
   C. Dr. Jerri Nielson loved Antarctica.
   D. Dr. Jerri Nielson was tired of being an emergency room doctor.

2. Answer the following questions.

   Where had Jerri worked before going to Antarctica?

   _____

   When did she discover the lump?

   _____

   When did she leave Antarctica?

   _____

   How long did the airplane stay on the ground when it stopped for Jerri?

   _____

3. Number the following events in the order they happened.

   _____ Jerri had surgery.

   _____ A plane dropped supplies to treat Jerri's cancer.
   _____ Jerri went to Antarctica.

   _____ Jerri came back from Antarctica.

   _____ Jerri discovered a lump in her breast.

4. What does the word **treatments** mean in the story?
   A. tests
   B. attempts to cure a disease
   C. supplies
   D. paintings

5. Why do you think Jerri Nielson chose to be a doctor in Antarctica?
   A. A job in Antarctica would be really different than working in an emergency room.
   B. She probably enjoyed snow and cold temperatures.
   C. Jerri couldn't help people in America.
   D. She wanted to be away from home for a long time.

Bonus:

Do you have what it takes to survive in Antarctica? Write about some of the characteristics you have that would help you survive.

Preventing Burns

Many people are severely burned each year. Many burn accidents involve children. However, a lot of burns that children suffer can be prevented.

The kitchen is a good place to start preventing burns. Small children should not be in the kitchen. Burns occur when children reach up to grab pot handles on a stove. Burns happen when cords from fryers and electric cookers are left hanging from a counter and children grab them. Pot handles should be turned in toward the stove, and cords should be placed on the counter away from small hands. Always keep potholders within reach, as they help prevent many burns in the kitchen.

Many burn survivors were using candles when their burns occurred. Candles can be decorative and smell great, but are dangerous when left **unattended**. Candles should never burn near a curtain or on uneven surfaces. Children should never be allowed near candles because the wax can cause serious injuries.

Many children are scalded each year in the bathtub or shower. Parents should test the water temperature before a child climbs in a shower or tub. Hot water burns are preventable when adults are supervising.

Many people who survive burns were warned of fires by smoke detectors. When a fire starts in your house, the smoke causes the alarm to sound. This gives a family a head start on getting out alive.

What if you get burned? Don't panic! Hold the burned area under running cold water for at least a minute and then wrap it in something clean and dry. If the burn is larger than a softball, call the doctor. Follow the tips above, and hopefully, you can avoid a major burn.

 CD-4320 Survivors: High-Interest Nonfiction

Surviving Burns

Many people are severely burned each year. Many burn accidents involve children. However, a lot of burns that children suffer can be prevented.

Start with making the kitchen safe. Small children should not be in the kitchen. Burns happen when children reach up to grab pot handles on a stove. They happen when cords from fryers and electric cookers are left hanging from a counter. Pot handles should be turned in toward the stove. Cords should be placed on the counter. Keep potholders within reach. They help prevent burns in the kitchen.

Candles look nice and smell great, but they are dangerous when left **unattended**. Don't use a candle near a curtain. Never burn one on an uneven surface. Children should never be allowed near candles. The wax can cause serious burns.

Many children are burned each year in the bathtub or shower. Parents should test the water before a child climbs in a shower or tub. Hot water burns are preventable. Adults should always supervise.

Smoke detectors help people survive. When a fire starts in a house, the smoke causes the alarm to sound. This gives a family a head start on getting out alive.

What if you get burned? Don't panic! Hold the burned area under running cold water for at least a minute. Then wrap it in something clean and dry. If the burn is larger than a softball, call the doctor. Follow the tips above, and hopefully, you can avoid a major burn.

Preventing Burns

1. What was the main idea of the second paragraph?
   A. Stoves cause many accidents.
   B. Children should never be in the kitchen.
   C. Many burns in the kitchen can be prevented.
   D. Using potholders can help prevent burns.

2. Answer the following questions.

   What should be within reach in the kitchen to help prevent burns?

   _____

   How can burns in the shower or bathtub be prevented?

   _____

   How do smoke detectors help people survive?

   _____

   What is the first thing you should do if you are burned?

   _____

3. Number the following events in the order they happened.

   _____ You call the doctor.

   _____ You check to see if the burn is larger than a softball.
   _____ You burn yourself severely.

   _____ You wrap the burn in something clean and dry.
   _____ You hold the burned area under running cold water for at least a minute.

4. What does the word **unattended** mean in the story?
   A. left outside
   B. left inside
   C. left on a shelf
   D. left alone

5. Why do you think you should hold a burned area under cold water for at least a minute?
   A. It makes the burn feel better.
   B. It helps the burned skin to stop burning.
   C. It cleans the area of the burn.
   D. All of the above.

Bonus:
Write a paragraph telling what things could be done in your home or classroom to prevent someone from getting burns.

49

Surviving Superhero

Superman began as a comic strip in 1939. Then, in 1978 the comic was made into a movie for the fourth time. Christopher Reeve played the superhero in the movie. Did you know that Christopher Reeve is a real-life survivor and hero, too?

Reeve has been acting since he was eight. He's taken many roles in his career. In London and Paris, he acted on stage. From 1974 to 1976, he played a part in a soap opera in the United States. Then, he got the starring role in *Superman*. It was one of his biggest roles. It was so popular that three sequels were made in later years.

Reeve kept pursuing his acting career through 1995. Then, in 1995 Reeve received one of the most challenging roles of his life.

He was riding in a horse race one afternoon. Everything was going well until his horse stumbled, and he fell headfirst off of the horse. When he fell, he broke a bone in his neck. This fall left him paralyzed from the neck down. A machine in his wheelchair helps him breathe. His doctors said he would never walk again.

Reeve considers the doctors' words a challenge. He continues to be positive about his **recovery**. He has even had some feeling return to his limbs. He believes he will walk again. Just a year after his accident he helped create a research facility. This facility researches spinal cord injuries. With research, he hopes to someday find a cure for spinal cord injuries.

He is an inspiration to everyone who has been faced with difficult challenges. He's shown the world how important it is to never give up on your dreams or lose hope. Reeve is a survivor and a hero for us all.

Surviving Superhero

Superman began as a comic strip in 1939. In 1978 the comic was made into a movie for the fourth time. Christopher Reeve played the superhero in the movie. Did you know that he is also a real-life survivor and hero?

Reeve has been acting since he was eight. He's taken many roles in his career. He's acted on stage. He's been on television. Then, he got the starring role in *Superman*. It was one of his biggest roles. Three more Superman movies were made later.

Then, in 1995, Reeve faced one of the hardest roles of his life.

He was riding in a horse race. Everything was going well. Then, his horse stumbled. Reeve fell off the horse headfirst. When he fell, he broke a bone in his neck. He was paralyzed from the neck down. To help him breathe, a machine was put in his wheelchair. His doctors said he would never walk again.

Reeve took the doctors' words as a challenge. He is positive about his **recovery**. Some feeling has even returned to his limbs. He knows he will walk again. Just a year after his fall, he helped create a place to do research. This lab researches spinal cord injuries. Someday, he hopes to find a cure.

Reeve is a role model to anyone who has faced tough problems. He's shown the world how important it is to never give up on your dreams or lose hope. Reeve is a survivor and a hero for us all.

 CD-4320 Survivors: High-Interest Nonfiction

Surviving Superhero

1. What was the main idea of the second paragraph?
   A. He liked acting on television.
   B. His favorite role was Superman.
   C. He did several kinds of acting.
   D. He liked performing on stage.

2. Answer the following questions.

   At what age did Reeve get his first acting role?

   _____

   Where did the idea for the movie *Superman* come from?

   _____

   When did Reeve have his accident?

   _____

   What did Reeve help create after his accident?

   _____

3. Number the following events in the order they happened.

   _____ Reeve acted in on stage.

   _____ Reeve got his first acting role.

   _____ Reeve created a research lab.

   _____ Reeve fell from his horse.

   _____ Doctors said he would not walk again.

4. What does the word **recovery** mean in the story?
   A. a new job
   B. healing
   C. not walking
   D. gaining strength

5. Why do you think Reeve took so many kinds of acting jobs in his career?
   A. He couldn't get any other kind of work.
   B. He was only good at acting on stage.
   C. He liked playing new characters.
   D. He was only good at acting in movies.

Bonus:
Write about another real-life "superhero" you know.

The Toughest Ride

Lance Armstrong was feeling like he was on top of the world. He had just won the World Cycling Championship. He was young, successful, and happy. What could possibly go wrong?

But then the unthinkable happened, and Lance became terribly ill. The doctors diagnosed him with cancer, and it was spreading quickly. They didn't think he would survive.

Lance had surgery, and then started chemotherapy treatments. Chemotherapy uses chemicals to try to stop cancer. It can make the patient feel very sick. Sometimes Lance was so ill he couldn't even watch television or read. However, eighteen months later Lance could say he beat the odds. He was cancer free!

After such a long, terrifying fight against death, Lance wasn't sure he could or even wanted to be a professional cycling champion again. But then, he entered his first cycling race since his illness. He only finished in fourteenth place. On his next race, the bad weather made him drop out on the second day. He was about to give up on cycling completely.

Lance's best friend decided to take him to the mountains of North Carolina to train. It was difficult but beautiful terrain. Lance had trained there before and liked it. After a challenging 5,000-foot ride up Beech Mountain, he felt like his old self. He remembered something his mother had always told him, "Make every obstacle an opportunity."

Lance was ready to **compete** again. After lots of hard training, he began to race and win again. Then, he entered the most difficult cycling race of all, the Tour de France. He won. Not just once, but four times in a row!

CD-4320 Survivors: High-Interest Nonfiction

The Toughest Ride

Lance Armstrong was on top of the world. He had just won the World Cycling Championship. He was young, successful, and happy. What could go wrong?

But then something terrible happened. Lance became very ill. The doctors told him he had cancer. It was spreading quickly. They didn't think he would live.

Lance had surgery. Then, he started chemotherapy treatments. Chemotherapy uses chemicals to try to stop cancer. It can make the patient feel very sick. Sometimes Lance was so ill he couldn't even watch television or read.

However, eighteen months later, Lance could say he beat the odds. He was cancer free!

But Lance wasn't sure he could or even wanted to be a cycling champion again. He entered his first race since his sickness. He only finished in fourteenth place. On his next race, it was cold and rainy. He dropped out on the second day. He didn't think he could do it anymore.

Lance's best friend took him to train in the North Carolina mountains. Lance had trained there before and liked it. After a tough 5,000-foot ride up Beech Mountain, he felt like his old self. He decided not to give up.

Lance was ready to **compete** again. After lots of hard training, he began to race and win again. Then, he entered the toughest race of all, the Tour de France. He won. Not just once, but four times in a row!

The Toughest Ride

Name: _____

1. Choose another title for this story.
   A. The Tour de France
   B. The Big Comeback
   C. Chemotherapy
   D. Beech Mountain

2. Answer the following questions.

   Why did Lance Armstrong stop cycling?

   _____

   What did the doctors think when they found that Lance had cancer?

   _____

   What major cycling championship did Lance win four years in a row?

   _____

   Where did Lance go to get his fighting spirit back?

   _____

3. Number the following events in the order they happened.

   _____ Lance had surgery.

   _____ Lance won the Tour de France.

   _____ Lance won the World Cycling Championship.
   _____ Lance was told he had cancer.

   _____ Lance dropped out of a race after the second day.

4. What does the word **compete** mean in the story?
   A. climb
   B. train
   C. cheer
   D. race

5. What conclusion can you make about becoming a cycling champion?
   A. It can make you ill.
   B. It takes hard work.
   C. You have to be tall and thin.
   D. You have to be an American.

Bonus:
Write about a time when you decided not to give up on something.

55

A City Survives

Can you imagine building a house on an island of sand? What if the sand was only four to eight feet above sea level? Well, that is exactly what 37,000 people did in the 1800s. That island city is Galveston, Texas.

Experts had said that Galveston was safe from storms. There had been several storms in Galveston that had resulted in very little damage. So people kept coming. People kept building. Then, on September 8, 1900, something unexpected happened.

A terrible hurricane hit the island. Thousands of people escaped over the bridge connecting Galveston to the mainland. Then, the bridge was underwater, too. Thousands of people had to stay on the island.

The winds were blowing at about 120 miles per hour. Every building was damaged. Most of the homes and buildings were swept away. The entire island was under the sea, and the water kept rising.

When the storm was over, it was dawn. The survivors couldn't believe what they saw. More than 6,000 people died, but over 30,000 people survived.

The hurricane was recorded as the worst natural **disaster** in United States history. But the people of Galveston decided to use what they learned. They rebuilt their island city. They raised the level of the city by bringing in more sand. They also built a seawall. It is 16 high and 17 feet thick. A hundred years after the storm, over 250,000 people called Galveston their home.

A City Survives

Would you build a house on an island made of sand? What if the sand was only a few feet above sea level? Well, that is just what 37,000 people did in the 1800s. That island city is Galveston, Texas.

Many people had said the island was safe. There had been a few storms before. They didn't do much harm. So people kept coming. People kept building. Then, on September 8, 1900, something bad happened.

A huge storm hit the island. Many people went to the mainland across a bridge. Then, the bridge was underwater, too. Thousands more people had to stay on the island.

The winds were blowing at about 120 miles per hour. Every building was damaged. Most of the homes and buildings were gone. The entire island was under the sea. But the water kept rising.

When the storm was over, it was dawn. The survivors couldn't believe what they saw. More than 6,000 people died, but over 30,000 people lived.

The hurricane was the worst natural **disaster** in United States history. But the people of Galveston wouldn't give up. They used what they learned. They rebuilt their island city. They also built a seawall. It is 16 feet high and 17 feet thick. In the year 2000, over 250,000 people called Galveston their home.

A City Survives

1. Choose another title for this story.
   A. An Island Paradise
   B. Hurricanes
   C. Building Seawalls
   D. Learning from Disaster

2. Answer the following questions.

   About how many people lived in Galveston in the year 2000?

   _____

   On what date did the hurricane hit Galveston?

   _____

   About how many people died in the hurricane?

   _____

   Galveston is off the coast of what state?

   _____

3. Number the following events in the order they happened.

   _____ The bridge was underwater.

   _____ Experts said Galveston didn't have to worry about hurricanes.
   _____ People built a seawall to protect the city.
   _____ The hurricane hit Galveston.

   _____ Thousands of people fled to the mainland.

4. What does the word **disaster** mean in this story?
   A. a serious mistake
   B. an event that causes great loss and destruction
   C. a bad storm
   D. a failure

5. Why do you think more people didn't try to leave the island?
   A. They wanted to see what happened.
   B. They liked watching storms.
   C. They waited too late, and the bridge was underwater.
   D. They'd survived worse natural disasters.

Bonus:

Write a paragraph to explain why you think people decided to come back and rebuild their city.

Crash Landing!

As a research scientist, Amy Knowlton normally dedicates herself to helping whales survive. But in January of 1987, she was fighting for her own life.

To get close to the whales, she and other scientists use airplanes. On this day, they were flying over the Atlantic Ocean about 40 miles from the coast of Georgia to see some whales and their new calves.

Amy and the other scientists took off and flew over the ocean. All of the gas tanks were filled before take-off. When the back-up tanks were almost out of gas, the pilot switched to the main gas tanks. There was a problem with the fuel switch, and soon both engines on the small plane died.

While the pilot tried to keep the plane in the air, Knowlton sent out a distress call. She had a marine radio, like a big walkie-talkie. She talked to the Coast Guard and told them where she thought they were.

The pilot instructed everyone to put on life jackets because they were going to crash into the water. He estimated they were about twelve miles from shore.

The plane hit the water and began filling. Immediately, they were up to their waists in cold water. Amy and the others had a difficult time opening the door. When they got it open, the water was up to their necks, and more water came pouring into the plane. One by one, Knowlton and the others swam out of the plane. The pilot came out last, after finding the life raft and checking that everyone had escaped.

Knowlton and the others **inflated** the life raft and climbed aboard. Over two hours later, the Coast Guard found them and brought them home. They are survivors because no one panicked. Amy's advice for anyone in a bad situation is to keep your cool.

Crash Landing!

A scientist named Amy Knowlton tries to help whales survive. But in January 1987, she was fighting for her own life.

To get close to the whales, she and other scientists use airplanes. On this day, they were flying over the Atlantic Ocean. They were about 40 miles from the coast of Georgia.

The gas tanks were full before take-off. But there was a problem with the tanks. Soon, both engines on the small plane died.

The pilot tried to keep the plane in the air. Knowlton sent out a distress call on the radio. She told the Coast Guard where she thought they were.

The pilot told everyone to put on life jackets. They were going to crash into the water. He guessed they were now about twelve miles from shore.

The plane hit the ocean and began filling with water. Amy and the others had a hard time opening the door. When they got it open, the cold water was up to their necks. One by one, Knowlton and the others swam out of the plane. The pilot came out last. He found the life raft and made sure that everyone was out of the plane.

Knowlton and the others **inflated** the life raft and climbed aboard. Over two hours later, the Coast Guard found them. They brought them home. Knowlton and the others are survivors because no one panicked. Amy now knows how important it is to always keep your cool.

Crash Landing!

Name: _____

1. What was the main idea of the third paragraph?
   A. Knowlton is a research scientist.
   B. The gas tanks were filled before take-off.
   C. They flew over the ocean to look for whales.
   D. As they were flying over the ocean, they found a problem with the tanks.

2. Answer the following questions.

   Where were the scientists flying to look for whales?

   _____

   Who sent out the distress call?

   _____

   Who was the last person out of the plane?

   _____

   Who rescued the crash survivors?

   _____

3. Number the following events in the order they happened.

   _____ The plane took off to fly over the ocean.
   _____ The pilot tried to keep the plane in the air.
   _____ There was a problem with the gas tanks.
   _____ They climbed aboard the life raft.
   _____ The plane hit the water.

4. What does the word **inflated** mean in the story?
   A. set up
   B. blew up
   C. poked
   D. painted

5. Why do you think it is important not to panic in an emergency situation?
   A. When you panic you don't think clearly and people can get hurt.
   B. When you panic everyone gets to safety more quickly.
   C. When you panic you take care of yourself first.
   D. When you panic other people around you become angry.

Bonus:
Write about a time when you or someone you know were in an emergency situation.

CD-4320 Survivors: High-Interest Nonfiction

Determination

One of the most popular singers today is a survivor. Gloria Estefan was born in Cuba in 1957. That was a time when many Cubans were fighting against their leader.

Gloria and her family had to **flee** Cuba to the United States. With little money, they had to live in a very poor section of Miami, Florida. Gloria's mother had to get a job to support the family while Gloria went to school and cared for her ailing father.

Gloria taught herself how to play the guitar when she was a young girl. Her future husband, Emilio Estefan, was impressed with Gloria's singing voice. He asked her to join his band. Gloria agreed to sing with his band but only on the weekends. She was determined to finish her college degree. That kind of focus would help her later.

She joined the band, called the Miami Sound Machine, and the rest is history. The group recorded songs in Spanish and English. In 1986, they had a hit song called "Conga" that was number one on the Pop, Latin, Soul and Dance charts all at the same time.

Everything was going well until March 20, 1990. The band was traveling on a tour bus. Gloria was napping in the back seat. Suddenly, a large semi truck hit the tour bus in the rear where Gloria was sleeping. She woke up on the floor. Gloria's back was broken.

She had surgery that required that two rods be placed in her back. She also had 400 stitches and months of pain.

But Gloria surprised her doctors. She was back on stage within a year. Her focus and determination served her well.

Determination

One of the most popular singers today is a survivor. Gloria Estefan was born in Cuba in 1957. That was a time when many Cubans were fighting against their leader.

Gloria and her family had to **flee** Cuba. With little money, they moved to a very poor part of Miami, Florida. Gloria went to school and cared for her sick father.

At age 12, Gloria was given a guitar. She taught herself how to play. A few years later, she met her future husband, Emilio. He loved Gloria's singing voice. He asked her to join his band. Gloria said yes, but only on the weekends. She wanted to finish college.

The band was called the Miami Sound Machine. The group sang songs in Spanish and English. They had many hit songs; especially one called "Conga."

Then, on March 20, 1990, the band was on a tour bus. A large truck hit the bus where Gloria was sleeping. She woke up on the floor. Her back was broken.

Gloria had surgery. The doctors put two rods in her back. She also had 400 stitches and months of pain.

But Gloria surprised her doctors. She was back on stage within a year. Nothing would stop her.

CD-4320 Survivors: High-Interest Nonfiction

Determination

1. The fifth paragraph is mainly about Gloria's
   A. singing career.
   B. accident.
   C. family.
   D. recovery.

2. Answer the following questions.

   In what languages did the Miami Sound Machine record their songs?

   _____

   Who taught Gloria to play the guitar?

   _____

   What did Gloria want to do before she became a full-time singer?

   _____

   How long was Gloria out recovering from her accident?

   _____

3. Number the following events in the order they happened.

   _____ Gloria received a guitar.

   _____ Gloria joined the Miami Sound Machine.

   _____ Gloria broke her back.

   _____ Gloria moved to Florida.

   _____ Gloria met her future husband.

4. What does the word **flee** mean in the story?
   A. leave quickly
   B. leave slowly
   C. compare
   D. prefer

5. Why did Gloria surprise her doctors?
   A. She took a long time to recover from her injury.
   B. Her music was different from what they expected.
   C. They didn't expect her to be back to work so quickly.
   D. She wanted more surgery.

Bonus:
Write about why you believe Gloria decided to finish her college degree before joining the band.

Fire and Water

Sidney and Dolly McTigue had a honeymoon to remember. The newlyweds were taking a relaxing trip to Cuba on the cruise ship *Morro Castle*. The year was 1934. Everything was great for the first few nights. But then, Sidney and Dolly awoke at three o'clock in the morning to the sound of screaming out in the hallway. Smoke was entering their cabin.

Somewhere on the ship, a fire had started in a closet. It quickly spread across the entire ship. There wasn't an alarm to warn anyone. Sidney and Dolly rushed outside to find the people panicking. No one had been told what to do in case of an emergency. There hadn't been a drill. Even the crew was at a loss for what to do.

The McTigues managed to find life preservers and jumped into the water from the top deck. It was a long drop. The water was freezing, but they thought it was better than being burned by the fire on the ship. A few lifeboats passed them by because they were too far away or too full.

Many people were floating around them in the water. At one point, a man yelled, "Sharks!" which created more **hysteria**. The waves were high, and Dolly and Sidney were exhausted, but they were determined to survive.

After spending seven hours in the water, they were almost too tired to stay afloat. But then a crowded lifeboat came into view. They swam to it, and Sidney forced their way onto the boat, despite the protests of the people already onboard. Many hours later, a large steamer arrived and plucked them out of the water. They were given warm clothing, blankets, and food. One hundred thirty-four people died that fateful night. The McTigues never went on a cruise again.

65

Fire and Water

Sidney and Dolly McTigue had a honeymoon they would never forget. The newlyweds were taking a trip to Cuba on the cruise ship *Morro Castle.* The year was 1934. Everything was great for the first few nights. But then, Sidney and Dolly awoke at three o'clock in the morning. There were people screaming out in the hallway. Smoke was entering their cabin.

Somewhere on the ship, a fire had started in a closet. It quickly spread across the whole ship. There wasn't an alarm. Sidney and Dolly rushed outside to find people panicking. They hadn't been told what to do in case of a fire. There had been no drill. Even the crew didn't know what to do.

Sidney and Dolly managed to find life preservers. They jumped into the water from the top deck. It was a long drop. The water was cold, too. They couldn't get on a lifeboat because the boats were too far away or too full.

Many people were around them in the water. Once, a man yelled, "Sharks!" This created more **hysteria**. The waves were high, and Sidney and Dolly were tired, but they weren't going to give up.

After seven hours in the water, they were almost too tired to keep floating. Then, Sidney and Dolly saw a crowded lifeboat. They swam to it. Sidney forced their way onto the boat. Many hours later, a large steam ship found them and lifted them out of the water. They were given warm clothing, blankets, and food. One hundred thirty-four people died. The McTigues never went on a cruise again.

Fire and Water

1. Choose another title for this story.
   A. A Cruise to Cuba
   B. The Sinking of the *Morro Castle*
   C. Wearing Life Preservers
   D. The Top Deck

2. Answer the following questions.

   Why were Sidney and Dolly taking a cruise?

   _____

   Why were people panicking when the fire started?

   _____

   How long were the McTigues in the water?

   _____

   What was the temperature of the water like?

   _____

3. Number the following events in the order they happened.

   _____ Sidney and Dolly jumped from the top deck.
   _____ The McTigues awoke to the sound of screams.
   _____ Sidney forced their way onto a lifeboat.
   _____ Sidney and Dolly began their honeymoon on the *Morro Castle*.
   _____ The McTigues were rescued by a large steam ship.

4. What does the word **hysteria** mean in the story?
   A. anger
   B. panic
   C. sadness
   D. worry

5. Why do you think the McTigues never went on a cruise again?
   A. The cabins were too small.
   B. There were never enough life boats.
   C. They didn't want to relive the terrible events of the *Morro Castle*.
   D. They knew the ship they went on would sink.

Bonus:
Write about why or why not you think having fire drills could have saved more lives on the *Morro Castle*.

Rose Freedman: Fire Survivor

Do you have an escape route if your home or school catches fire? What if you didn't? What if you were in a burning building and all of the doors were locked so you couldn't get out? On March 25, 1911, the Triangle Shirtwaist Factory in New York City caught on fire. All the workers were trapped inside.

But one woman managed to escape. Her name was Rose Freedman. After moving to America from Austria in 1909, she found a job making shirts at the Triangle Shirtwaist Factory.

The factory wasn't a very clean or safe place to work. A year after Rose got her job, the workers in the factory went on strike. They would not work until owners cleaned the workrooms and provided more safety precautions. The owners met only a few of the demands. But most of the workers couldn't afford to strike. They had to go back to work.

Then, on March 25, 1911, tragedy struck when a fire started at the factory. One hundred forty-six young people died that day. The workers had no way out of the factory. All the doors leading to stairways and fire escapes were locked. They were locked to prevent workers from leaving for breaks and stealing fabric. The only way out of the building was to jump seventy feet to the ground.

Rose Freedman was the only survivor. She managed to find some stairs, and then raced to the roof. When she looked down, she noticed that the firefighters were more interested in **dousing** the blaze than helping workers escape.

Rose saved her own life by keeping calm. She jumped to the roof of another building and hurried down ten flights of stairs to safety. She was offered a bribe to tell others that the fire escape doors were open during the fire, but she refused. Because of the testimony of Rose Freedman, safety laws were created to prevent tragedies like this one. Many of these laws still exist today. Rose Freedman lived to the age of 107.

Rose Freedman: Fire Survivor

What if you were in a burning building and all of the doors were locked so you couldn't get out? On March 25, 1911, the Triangle Shirtwaist Factory in New York City caught on fire. All the workers were trapped inside.

But one woman managed to escape. Her name was Rose Freedman. She found a job making shirts at the Triangle Shirtwaist Factory. She had just moved to America from Austria in 1909.

The factory wasn't a very clean place to work. It wasn't safe either. The workers in the factory went on strike. They would not work until owners cleaned the workrooms and made it safer. The owners met only a few of the demands. But most of the workers needed money. They had to go back to work.

Then, on March 25, 1911, a fire started in the factory. One hundred forty-six young people died that day. They had no way out of the factory. All of the doors were locked. They were locked to keep workers from taking breaks and stealing fabric. The only way out was to jump seventy feet to the ground.

Rose Freedman was the only survivor. She managed to find some stairs, and then she ran to the roof. When she looked down, she saw that the firemen were **dousing** the blaze. They weren't helping workers escape.

Rose saved her own life by keeping calm. She jumped to the roof of another building. Then, she hurried down ten flights of stairs to safety. After the fire, she was offered money. They wanted her to say that the fire escape doors were open during the fire. Rose refused. Because Rose Freedman told the truth, laws were made to make factories safer. Many of these laws still exist today. Rose Freedman lived to the age of 107.

CD-4320 Survivors: High-Interest Nonfiction

Rose Freedman

Name: _____

1. What was the main idea of the third paragraph?
   A. Workers wanted cleaner and safer working conditions.
   B. The owners met few of their demands.
   C. Most workers couldn't afford to strike.
   D. Workers wanted new jobs.

2. Answer the following questions.

   What country did Rose live in before moving to America?

   _____

   On what date did the fire take place?

   _____

   What did Freedman do when she was offered a bribe?

   _____

   Why were workers in the factory trapped?

   _____

3. Number the following events in the order they happened.

   _____ Rose got a job making shirts.

   _____ The workers went on strike.

   _____ New safety laws were created.

   _____ A fire broke out at the factory.

   _____ Rose moved to New York.

4. What does the word **dousing** mean in the story?
   A. fanning
   B. lighting
   C. putting out
   D. helping

5. Why do you think Rose refused to lie about the fire escape doors being open?
   A. They didn't offer her enough money to lie.
   B. She wanted to make the business owners happy.
   C. Her friends told her not to lie.
   D. She wanted people to know about the poor working conditions of the factory.

Bonus:
Do you and your family have a fire escape plan in place for your home? Write directions describing your plan or create one you would like to have for your family.

Shaky Ground

It was early morning, and most people were still asleep. Emma Burke and her husband had just climbed out of bed. Suddenly, the ground shifted so violently it threw the bed against the wall. They knew it was an earthquake.

The rumble of the shaking got louder and louder. The Burkes stood in the doorway to avoid the things falling around them. Gradually, the shaking stopped. They could hear crying from the street.

The infamous San Francisco earthquake of 1906 had lasted a scary 48 seconds. The Burkes got dressed and left their home several minutes later.

The damage was frightening. The Burkes walked for an hour to look at the **destruction**. After seeing many people with nothing left, the Burkes knew they were lucky. Their home was still standing. After gathering some things from their home, the Burkes spent hours feeding people who had lost everything.

Because it was too dangerous to sleep in their homes, many slept outside. The Burkes took blankets to a park and slept under a tree. During the night, they began to notice huge fires burning through San Francisco. People were being called to new jobs as firefighters and even bakers. There were going to be many hungry people in the morning.

After the first night, Mr. Burke was put in charge of giving out fresh water. Mrs. Burke fed the homeless and the hungry until her own food was gone. She didn't turn anyone away until all the food from her home had been eaten.

The one thing the Burkes noticed during this disaster was people helping people. Before the earthquake, most had taken care of themselves and their families. After the earthquake, people worked together to survive.

71

Shaky Ground

It was early morning. Most people were still asleep. Emma Burke and her husband had just climbed out of bed. The ground began shaking beneath them. It was an earthquake!

The rumble from the shaking was very loud. The Burkes stood in the doorway. They knew this was the safest place. Things were falling all around them. Slowly, the shaking stopped. They could hear crying from the street.

The San Francisco earthquake of 1906 lasted 48 seconds. The Burkes put on warm clothes. They left their home a few minutes later.

The damage was bad. The Burkes walked for an hour to look at the **destruction**. After seeing many people with nothing left, they knew they were lucky. Their home was still standing. So, the Burkes gathered some things from their home. Then, they spent hours feeding people who had lost everything.

It was too risky to sleep in their home. The Burkes took blankets and pillows to a park and slept under a tree. During the night they saw huge fires burning. People were getting new jobs as firefighters and bakers. There were going to be hungry people in the morning.

Mr. Burke was put in charge of giving out fresh water. Long lines of people waited all day for a drink. Mrs. Burke fed people until all the food in their house was gone. She didn't turn anyone away until all the food from her home had been eaten.

The Burkes noticed one thing during this disaster. Before the earthquake most people had taken care of themselves and their families. After the earthquake, people worked together to survive.

Shaky Ground

1. What was the main idea of the last paragraph?
   A. When disaster strikes, people help each other.
   B. If you lose everything in an earthquake, some people will help you.
   C. Earthquakes are terrible disasters.
   D. The Burkes were very nice people.

2. Answer the following questions.

   How long did the earthquake last?
   _____

   Who was the story about?
   _____

   Where did the earthquake happen?
   _____

   At what time of day did the earthquake happen?
   _____

3. Number the following events in the order they happened.

   _____ Mr. Burke was placed in charge of giving out fresh water.
   _____ The Burkes stood in the doorway during the earthquake.
   _____ People became bakers and fire-fighters during the night.
   _____ The Burkes decided to sleep at the park.
   _____ Mrs. Burke fed people until she ran out of food.

4. What does the word **destruction** mean in the story?
   A. new homes
   B. people
   C. confusion
   D. damage

5. Why was it too dangerous to sleep inside after the earthquake?
   A. They were afraid someone might come to rob their house.
   B. They worried that their house might fall down because of earthquake damage.
   C. They were worried about leaking water pipes.
   D. They were worried about a storm coming.

Bonus:
Write about why you think the Burkes were lucky during this disaster.

73

Unsinkable Survivor

History remembers her as the "Unsinkable Molly Brown." She survived the sinking of the cruise ship *Titanic*. Only 705 people survived that cold night out of 2,200 people onboard. The facts of Brown's life have almost become legendary, even though some of these facts have been exaggerated.

Her real name was Margaret "Maggie" Tobin. The nickname "Molly" was made up in Hollywood after she died. Maggie grew up in Missouri near the Mississippi River. Her family was poor and lived in a one-bedroom house. She wanted adventure and wealth. When she was a teenager, she went to work. She had a job at a hotel for a while. Then she and her brother left their home to make their fortune. They went to Colorado to "strike it rich" with gold.

Maggie had a **vivid** imagination. This is probably why her story has grown. She claimed to be friends with the author Mark Twain as a child. She told all who would listen about being robbed by the famous outlaw Jesse James on her way to Colorado. These stories may not be true, but Maggie was a very strong person. This helped save her life on the night *Titanic* sank.

Maggie met and married J. J. Brown in Colorado. He was an engineer who mined for gold. When he found gold, the Browns became

instantly wealthy. They threw great parties and tried to impress other rich people. Soon they began traveling. Eventually, Maggie booked passage on the *Titanic*.

On the night of April 14, 1912, the supposedly "unsinkable" *Titanic* hit a large iceberg and sank into the cold, Arctic waters. The crewman in charge of Maggie's lifeboat decided that it was useless to try to save themselves. But Maggie wouldn't let them give up. She took command of the boat and saved herself and 14 others. She made them row to keep warm and kept their spirits high until the rescue boat arrived. Then, she helped organize rescues and made lists of survivors. She also got donations to help the survivors who didn't have much money.

She got her famous nickname by saying, "Typical Brown luck. We're unsinkable." She was a true survivor.

Unsinkable Survivor

S he is known as the "Unsinkable Molly Brown." She lived through the sinking of the ship *Titanic*. Only 705 people survived that cold night. Over 2,000 people were onboard. Brown's life has almost become a legend. Some stories about her might be made up, though.

Margaret "Maggie" Tobin never used the name "Molly." The nickname was invented in Hollywood after she died. She grew up in Missouri near the Mississippi River. Her family was poor. They lived in a one-bedroom house. She wanted adventure and money. When she was a teenager, she went to work. She had a job at a hotel for a while. Then, she and her brother went to Colorado to find gold.

Maggie had a **vivid** imagination. Maybe this is why her story has grown. She said she was friends with the author Mark Twain. She said the famous outlaw Jesse James robbed her. These stories may not be true, but Maggie was a very strong person. This helped save her life on the night *Titanic* sank.

She met and married J. J. Brown in Colorado. He mined for gold. When he found gold, the Browns were rich. They threw great parties. They tried to impress other rich people. Soon, they began traveling. Maggie booked a trip on the *Titanic*.

On the night of April 14, 1912, the *Titanic* hit a large iceberg. It sank into the cold, Arctic waters. The crewman in charge of Maggie's lifeboat said it was useless to try to save themselves. But Maggie wouldn't let them give up.

She took over the boat and saved herself and 14 others. She made them row to keep warm. She kept their spirits high until the rescue boat arrived. Then, she helped with rescues and made lists of survivors. She also got money from rich survivors to help the poor ones.

She got her famous nickname by saying, "Typical Brown luck. We're unsinkable." She was a true survivor.

75

Unsinkable Survivor

1. What was the main idea of the second paragraph?
   A. She wanted to meet Mark Twain.
   B. She was poor as a child and then went to Colorado to get rich.
   C. Her family lived in a small house when she was young.
   D. Her name wasn't really "Molly."

2. Answer the following questions.

   When did the *Titanic* sink?

   _____

   What was Molly Brown's real name?

   _____

   Who did she marry?

   _____

   What did she do to help the people on her lifeboat keep warm?

   _____

3. Number the following events in the order they happened.

   _____ She sailed on the *Titanic*.

   _____ She married J. J. Brown.

   _____ She helped with the rescues.

   _____ She went to Colorado to get rich.

   _____ Margaret Tobin worked in a hotel.

4. What does the word **vivid** mean in the story?
   A. poor
   B. brilliant
   C. small
   D. dark

5. Why do you think Maggie was such a strong person?
   A. She had to be strong to meet her goals of being rich someday.
   B. She lifted weights as a child.
   C. A tragedy like the *Titanic* makes everyone strong.
   D. She had an imagination.

Bonus:

Suppose you could send a message back in time to Maggie Brown before she sailed on the *Titanic*. What would you say in your message? Would you warn her not to go on the ship? Explain why or why not.

After the Horror

Wiesel was taken to Paris where he spent a few years in a French orphanage. In 1948, he began college. He soon became a well-known journalist. For many years, Wiesel refused to talk about what had happened to him. He had lost his faith. A friend finally talked him into writing about what had happened.

Wiesel has since published over forty books. He has also earned the Nobel Peace Prize and been awarded the Congressional Gold Medal. Wiesel gives speeches around the world. He talks about the Jews and other groups who have suffered **persecution**. Wiesel wants to make sure none of us forget what happened during the Holocaust.

E lie Wiesel survived one of the worst events in modern history. It was called the Holocaust.

Elie was born in 1928 in a town that is now part of Romania. He had a very happy childhood until World War II began. At the age of fifteen, Wiesel, his family, and other Jews were sent to German concentration camps. This is where Jews were murdered, tortured, and starved. His mother and youngest sister were killed almost immediately. His father died later. In April 1945, the United States Army came into their camp and freed them. Wiesel and his two older sisters survived.

© Carson-Dellosa

After the Horror

Elie Wiesel lived through one of the worst events in modern times. It was called the Holocaust.

Elie was born in 1928. He lived in a town that is now part of Romania. He had a very happy childhood until World War II began. At the age of fifteen, Wiesel, his family, and other Jews were sent to German death camps. This is where Jews were murdered, tortured, and starved. His mother and youngest sister were killed almost immediately. His father died later. In April 1945, the United States Army came into their camp and freed them. Wiesel and his two older sisters survived.

Wiesel went to Paris. He became a reporter. For many years, Wiesel wouldn't talk about what had happened to him. He had lost his faith. A friend finally talked him into writing about what had happened.

Wiesel has since written over forty books. He has also earned the Nobel Peace Prize and the Congressional Gold Medal. Wiesel gives speeches around the world. He talks about the Jews and other victims of **persecution**. Wiesel wants to make sure none of us forget the Holocaust.

After the Horror

Name: _____

1. Choose another title for this story.
   A. Holocaust Survivor
   B. The Nobel Peace Prize
   C. The German Death Camps
   D. The Novels of Elie Wiesel

2. Answer the following questions.

   What was Wiesel's childhood like before World War II?

   _____

   How old was Wiesel when he and his family were taken to the death camps?

   _____

   To what city did Wiesel go after the war?

   _____

   About how many books has Wiesel written?

   _____

3. Number the following events in the order they happened.

   _____ Wiesel became a reporter.

   _____ Wiesel's mother and younger sister were killed.

   _____ The United States Army freed the Jews in the camp.

   _____ Wiesel and his family were sent to the German death camps.

   _____ The Nobel Peace Prize was awarded to Wiesel.

4. What does the word **persecution** mean in the story?
   A. cruelty
   B. weapons
   C. grief
   D. fear

5. Why do you think Wiesel wouldn't talk about what had happened to him at first?
   A. He didn't want anyone to know about what he'd lived through.
   B. He thought the German death camps should be kept secret.
   C. It was painful for him to talk about because it was so horrible.
   D. He didn't want to upset people.

Bonus:
Write about the importance of keeping the memory of the Holocaust alive.

     CD-4320 Survivors: High-Interest Nonfiction

A Lesson for the World

What would it be like to hide in a tiny attic for two years from people who wanted to kill you? What if you could never go outside and play? You can read such a story in *The Diary of Anne Frank.*

The world was a different place when Anne Frank was born in 1929. Anne and her family were Jewish and lived in Germany. When she was four years old, her family moved to Holland to escape the Nazis. But then Germany invaded Holland in 1940. Her family had to hide because the Nazis were doing terrible things to Jewish people. They hid themselves in a secret house for 25 months.

During this time, Anne received a diary for her sixteenth birthday. She began writing her thoughts about the war. She described her life with the eight other people who were hiding with her in the cramped attic. They had to be very quiet during the day. They didn't want people in the business below to hear them.

Anne wrote that for the world to survive, we must learn to respect one another. She knew people had to accept differences in others. As she wrote, she had no idea how her words would survive to affect future generations.

Anne and her family were captured on August 4, 1944. Anne did not survive, but her father did. He found her diary and **published** it in 1947. It has been printed in over sixty languages. Teachers around the world now use *The Diary of Anne Frank* to teach about humanity and respect.

Anne Frank's words still give us hope. Even though her life ended in tragedy, she still believed that people were truly good at heart.

A Lesson for the World

Anne wrote that we must learn to respect each other. She knew people had to accept others who are different.

The Nazis found Anne and her family on August 4, 1944. Anne didn't survive, but her father did. He found her diary and **published** it in 1947. It has been printed in over sixty languages. Teachers around the world now teach *The Diary of Anne Frank* to their students.

Anne Frank's words still give us hope. She felt that people were good at heart. Although she didn't survive the war, her diary and ideals did.

What would it be like to have to hide for two years? What if you could never play outside? You can read a story like this in *The Diary of Anne Frank*.

Anne Frank was born in 1929. Anne and her family were Jewish. They wanted to escape the Nazis. The Nazis were Germans who did awful things to Jews. Her family had to hide. They hid themselves in a secret attic for 25 months.

During this time, Anne got a diary. It was a birthday gift. She wrote in it about the war. She also told about what it was like to hide. Her family had to be very quiet during the daytime. They didn't want the people downstairs to hear them.

A Lesson for the World

1. What was the main idea of the third paragraph?
   A. Anne and her family were Jewish.
   B. Anne Frank wrote in her diary about life in the attic.
   C. Her diary was printed in over sixty languages.
   D. Her family had to be quiet during the day.

2. Answer the following questions.

   Why did Anne's family have to hide?

   _____

   Why did she get the diary?

   _____

   When was the diary published?

   _____

   Why did her family have to be quiet during the day?

   _____

3. Number the following events in the order they happened.

   _____ The diary was published.

   _____ Anne wrote about the war and her life of hiding.

   _____ Anne and her family had to hide from the Nazis.

   _____ Anne got a diary for her birthday.

   _____ Anne was born in 1929.

4. What does the word **published** mean?
   A. punished
   B. burned
   C. printed
   D. lost

5. Why do you think so many people read her diary?
   A. People want to learn about Anne Frank.
   B. People want to learn about the life of Jews during World War II.
   C. There are many lessons about life in the book.
   D. All of the above.

Bonus:

Write several diary entries of your own about how you would feel if you had to hide because of your beliefs.

Let Freedom Ring

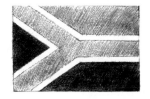

Before 1994, South Africa was not a free land. The black people of this country were separated from white people. This was called "apartheid" (a-par-tide). It meant that the government separated people by race.

White people enjoyed most of the rights in the country. Only they were allowed to vote. Black people also had their travel **restricted**. They couldn't move freely within their own country without passes. If they were caught without a pass, they were put in jail. They were even told where to live. But all of this changed with the efforts of Nelson Mandela.

Mandela was born in 1918. When Mandela was 12, his father died. A Thembu chief took care of him. He made sure that Nelson went to a good school.

By the time Mandela was 23, he was fighting against apartheid. He became a lawyer and helped set up South Africa's first black law firm in 1952. He was also a member of the African National Congress who fought for changes in laws for black people. The government outlawed this group, but Mandela continued his fight in hiding.

In 1962, Mandela was sent to prison for leaving the country illegally. Two years later, he was put on trial again for trying to take over the government. He was sent to prison for life.

But Nelson Mandela did not give up. He survived prison life by being friendly to the guards. He also made friends with people in the government.

In the 1980s, slow changes began to take place. Other countries wanted South Africa to treat black people better. Finally, in 1990, Nelson Mandela was released from jail. He had spent 27 years behind bars.

Mandela won the Nobel Peace Prize in 1993. A year later, South Africans had their first free election. Nelson Mandela became the first black president of South Africa. Mandela had survived injustice for many years. Now he and his people are free.

CD-4320 Survivors: High-Interest Nonfiction

Let Freedom Ring

Before 1994, South Africa was not a free land. The black people of this country were kept apart from white people. This was called "apartheid" (a-par-tide). It meant that the government separated people by race.

Black people didn't have many rights. Only white people could vote. Black people also had their travel **restricted**. They needed passes to move around within their own country. If they didn't have a pass, they were put in jail. Black people were even told where to live. But a man named Nelson Mandela helped change this.

Mandela was born in 1918. When Mandela was 12, his father died. A chief took care of him. He made sure that Nelson went to a good school.

When he was 23 years old, Mandela started fighting against apartheid. He became a lawyer. He tried to change the laws for black people. The government wouldn't let him. Mandela kept trying anyway.

In 1962, Mandela was sent to jail. He'd left the country without a pass. Two years later, he was on trial again for trying to take over the government. He was sent to jail for life.

But Nelson Mandela didn't give up. He survived prison life. He made friends with the guards and people in the government.

In the 1980s, changes began to take place. Other countries wanted South Africa to treat black people better. Finally, in 1990, Nelson Mandela was freed. He had spent 27 years in jail.

Mandela won the Nobel Peace Prize in 1993. A year later, South Africans voted in their first free election. Nelson Mandela became the first black president of South Africa. Mandela had survived injustice for many years. Now he and his people are free.

Let Freedom Ring

1. What was the main idea of the second paragraph?
   A. Nelson Mandela was born in 1918.
   B. Black people could not vote.
   C. Black people could not travel freely.
   D. Black people didn't have the same rights as white people in South Africa.

2. Answer the following questions.

   What does apartheid mean?
   _____

   Why was Mandela first put in jail?
   _____

   How long was he in jail?
   _____

   When did Nelson Mandela become president?
   _____

3. Number the following events in the order they happened.

   _____ Nelson Mandela became president.

   _____ Mandela was put in jail.

   _____ Mandela's father died.

   _____ Mandela became a lawyer.

   _____ Mandela was released from jail.

4. What does the word **restricted** mean in the story?
   A. helped
   B. limited
   C. angered
   D. terrified

5. Why do you think Mandela was finally let out of prison even though he was sentenced to life in jail?
   A. The prison ran out of room.
   B. They forgot that he was sentenced to life.
   C. The government wanted to show that it was changing the way it treated black people.
   D. Mandela talked the guards into letting him go.

Bonus:
Imagine that a bully makes you get permission from him whenever you want to leave your house. Write a story about what this might be like. How would this be similar to what black people lived through in South Africa?

85

Remembered

One way to survive is to be remembered. One way to be remembered is to have a holiday named in your honor. In the year 2000, the California governor declared March 31 a state holiday. It celebrates César Chávez's birthday.

César Chávez was born to poor **migrant** workers on a farm in Arizona. He lived in paper shacks and moved from farm to farm with his family. He saw the hard working conditions that his family and friends had to endure. It was a dangerous job, too. The fields they worked in were often sprayed with pesticides and poisons. But they had to work 12- to 14-hour days in those fields and were paid only enough to live.

Because his family moved so often, Chávez couldn't get a good education. Even though he could barely read and write, he had to drop out of school. As a young man, he watched his father and uncle join a labor union to fight for the rights of migrant farmers. Labor unions are groups of workers who stand up for better working conditions and wages.

After Chávez served in the United States Navy during World War II, he returned to his family. Conditions had not improved. He decided to dedicate his life to helping migrant workers and their families.

Chávez volunteered and worked for several labor unions but then decided to start his own. It is called the United Farm Workers Union (UFW). His members used nonviolent tactics. For example, they organized hunger strikes, church services, and marches.

Chávez did much to improve the lives of farm workers. He got them higher pay. He also gave them a better, healthier way of life. Even after his death in 1993, his work still goes on. He is gone but not forgotten.

Remembered

No one will forget a man named César Chávez. Now there's even a holiday for him in California. It's on March 31, his birthday.

Chávez was born to poor **migrant** workers on a farm in Arizona. His family moved from farm to farm and lived in shacks. He saw the hard work his family and friends had to do in the fields. They were paid only enough to live. It wasn't a safe job either. The fields were often sprayed with poisons. But they worked 12- to 14-hour days in those fields.

Because his family moved so much, Chávez had to drop out of school. He could barely read and write. As a young man, he saw his father and uncle join a labor union. They fought for better working conditions and pay. Chávez learned a lot from this.

Chávez spent two years in the United States Navy. Then, he went home to his family. Things had not improved. He then decided to help farm workers and their families.

Chávez worked for several labor unions but then decided to start his own. It is called the United Farm Workers Union (UFW). His members believed in nonviolence. For example, they organized hunger strikes, church services, and marches to get what they wanted.

César Chávez did much to improve the lives of farm workers. He got them higher pay. He also gave them a better, healthier way of life. Even after his death in 1993, his work still goes on. He is gone but not forgotten.

Remembered

1. Choose another title for this story.
   A. Holidays
   B. Farming
   C. Stay in School
   D. A Peaceful Leader

2. Answer the following questions.

   What is the UFW?

   _____

   How many hours in the day did migrant workers have to work?

   _____

   What date is the César Chávez holiday?

   _____

   Why was working in the field unsafe?

   _____

3. Number the following events in the order they happened.

   _____ Chávez joins the United States Navy.

   _____ Chávez drops out of school.

   _____ Chávez starts the United Farm Workers Union.

   _____ California observes a César Chávez holiday.

   _____ Chávez gets migrant workers higher pay.

4. What does the word **migrant** mean in the story?
   A. moving
   B. happy
   C. hungry
   D. careful

5. Why do you think Chávez had to drop out of school?
   A. He wasn't very smart and didn't want to learn.
   B. He had a behavioral problem.
   C. He changed schools so often that he felt like he got too far behind to catch up.
   D. He couldn't read or write.

Bonus:

César Chávez once said, "Nonviolence is hard work. It is the willingness to sacrifice. It is the patience to win." Write a paragraph explaining what this quote means to you.

Surviving Hatred

Have you ever not wanted to go to school? What if you knew that when you got to school, adults would be shaking their fists and yelling at you to go home? What if you were only six years old when this happened?

That happened to Ruby Bridges on November 14, 1960. That was the day the public schools in New Orleans became **integrated**. Ruby was the first African-American child to attend a once all-white elementary school.

Ruby's parents wanted her to go to a good school. The best school with the best teachers was just five blocks away from their home. However, it was an all-white school. It took a new law, a court order, and lots of police officers to see that Ruby could start going to that school.

The people in that Louisiana city weren't happy. They didn't like the change and tried to get Ruby to stay home. People made threats on her family members' lives. Ruby's father was fired from his job.

On that first day of school, Ruby waited in the principal's office all day. On her second day, she met her teacher, Mrs. Henry, and entered her classroom. The white parents had kept their children home. Ruby was Mrs. Henry's only student all year.

Nevertheless, Ruby finished her schooling and became a successful businessperson. She even helps out at the school she helped integrate. Ruby is proud to have survived the hatred of those times. She knows that, because of it all, children today have a chance for an equal education.

89

Surviving Hatred

Have you ever not wanted to go to school? What if you knew that when you got to school, adults would be yelling at you to go home? What if you were only six years old when this happened?

That happened to Ruby Bridges on November 14, 1960. That was the day the public schools in New Orleans were **integrated**. Ruby was the first African-American child to go to an elementary school that was once for white people only.

Ruby's parents wanted her to go to a good school. The best school was just five blocks away from their home. However, it was only for white students. It took a new law, an order from a judge, and lots of police officers to see that Ruby could start going to that school.

The people in that city weren't happy. They tried to get Ruby to stay home. People made threats on her family members' lives. Ruby's father was fired from his job.

On that first day, Ruby waited in an office all day. On her second day, she went to her classroom. She met her teacher, Mrs. Henry. The white parents had kept their children home. Ruby was Mrs. Henry's only student all year.

Ruby worked hard and got good grades. She grew up and went into business. She even helps out at her old school. Ruby is proud to have survived those times. She knows that what she did helped all children today have chance for a better education.

Surviving Hatred

1. Choose another title for this story.
   A. Equal Education for All
   B. Good Schools Are Hard to Find
   C. Study Hard and You Will Do Well
   D. Some People Can Be Mean

2. Answer the following questions.

   How far away did Ruby live from the school her parents wanted her to attend?

   _____

   In what city did Ruby live?

   _____

   What happened to Ruby's father when she started at the new school?

   _____

   How many classmates attended class with Ruby and Mrs. Henry?

   _____

3. Number the following events in the order they happened.

   _____ A law was passed integrating public schools.
   _____ Ruby entered an all-white school.

   _____ Ruby waited in the principal's office on her first day of school.
   _____ Ruby went to business school.

   _____ Ruby met Mrs. Henry.

4. What does the word **integrated** mean in the story?
   A. mixed
   B. separated
   C. decided
   D. helped

5. What conclusions can you draw about Ruby from the story?
   A. She was angry.
   B. She was brave.
   C. She was already reading.
   D. She liked her teacher.

Bonus:
Imagine Ruby Bridges was still six years old and starting at her new school. If you wrote a letter to her, what would you say?

© Carson-Dellosa   CD-4320 Survivors: High-Interest Nonfiction

Vietnamese War Orphans

On a spring evening in 1975, a 16-year-old boy ran for his life. His country, Vietnam, was overtaken by an enemy. Bullets were flying, and bombs were blasting everywhere he turned. He ran to the sea and lay down on the floor of a fishing boat. He thought his life was over.

Nghi Si Do, along with over one hundred other Vietnamese orphans, was hoping to escape on that tiny vessel. A few miles off the coast, the engine stopped. Nghi Si Do was afraid, exhausted, and out of hope. He did the only thing he could think to do. He went to sleep.

When he awoke, he was amazed to find that a large ship had discovered them and towed them to safety in Singapore. There, a missionary took in the entire group, sponsored them, and flew them to America. They stayed at an orphanage in Texas. All survived the horrible night.

Mr. Do married one of the survivors and they now have two teenage daughters. He became an accountant and still lives in Texas.

Every year, the survivors gather in Dallas to remember their experience. Soon, the reunion will be held in Vietnam. Mr. Do says he doesn't **dwell** on the past. He says as horrible as that night was, he thinks about how lucky he was to survive and become a citizen of the United States.

Vietnamese War Orphans

On a spring night in 1975, a 16-year-old boy ran for his life. His country, Vietnam, was falling into the hands of an enemy. Bullets were flying, and bombs were blasting everywhere he turned. He ran to the sea and lay down on the floor of a fishing boat. He thought his life was over.

Nghi Si Do was hoping to escape on that tiny boat. Over one hundred other Vietnamese orphans were on it with him. Suddenly the boat's engine stopped. They were a few miles off the coast. Nghi Si Do was scared, tired, and out of hope. The only thing he could do was sleep.

When he awoke, he learned that a large ship had found them. It towed them to safety in Singapore. There, a missionary found a way to get the orphans safely to America. They stayed at an orphanage in Texas. All of them survived the horrible night.

Mr. Do married one of the survivors. They now have two teenage daughters. He became an accountant. They still live in Texas.

Every year, the survivors meet in Dallas. They want to remember their experience. Soon, they'll meet in Vietnam. Mr. Do says he doesn't **dwell** on the past. Instead, he thinks about how lucky he was to survive. He's thankful that he became a citizen of the United States.

CD-4320 Survivors: High-Interest Nonfiction

Name: _____

1. Choose another title for this passage.
   A. Old Friends
   B. A Trip to Dallas
   C. Escape!
   D. Long Lost Parents

2. Answer the following questions.

   Where did the surviving orphans meet every year?

   _____

   How many orphans survived their escape?

   _____

   What job does Nghi Si Do have in the United States?

   _____

   How old was Nghi Si Do when he escaped from Vietnam?

   _____

3. Number the following events in the order they happened.

   _____ A missionary sent the orphans to the United States.

   _____ Nghi Si Do married another survivor.

   _____ Bullets were flying everywhere.

   _____ Nghi Si Do hid on a fishing boat.

   _____ The orphans meet every year.

4. What does the word **dwell** mean in the story?
   A. to forget
   B. to think about for a long time
   C. to stay with
   D. to live in a house

5. What do you think happened to Mr. Do's parents?
   A. He met them in Dallas.
   B. They sent them to live with relatives.
   C. They moved to Singapore.
   D. He lost them in Vietnam.

Bonus:
Nghi Si Do and the other orphans are planning a return trip to Vietnam. Write a paragraph about how you think they will feel when they get there.

Bear-Be-Gone!

Have you ever heard of mace? It's a spray police officers use to **restrain** criminals. Some people carry mace to defend themselves. When sprayed in the face, attackers are in too much pain to fight back. Now, there is a spray especially for bears, and it helped one man and his friends survive a bear attack.

Pat Goodwin and four of his friends went backpacking on Kodiak Island in Alaska. They knew the island had bears but chose not to take any guns for protection. His friend Todd had purchased a can of pepper spray for bears. Goodwin and his friends laughed and told Todd that he had wasted his money. As it turned out, the can of pepper spray saved their lives.

On the last day of their camping trip, they were heading down a trail and saw a bear and its baby. Pat was yelling at the others to come and see the bears, as he excitedly took out his camera to get a picture. Then, the mother bear, called a sow, sniffed the air and began charging up the trail toward the hikers. Pat turned and ran, shouting at his friends to run. The hikers ran until they were cornered. The sow, wanting to protect her baby, approached the terrified group slowly, growling and snorting.

When the bear was 15 feet away, Pat tried to light a flare to throw at her, but it didn't work. Then, Todd came to the rescue with his pepper spray. He sprayed the sow with a fog of pepper spray. The bear pawed at her head, sneezing, and snorting, and then ran off. The pepper spray helped Pat, Todd, and their friends survive. It also saved the bear. If they had brought a gun instead of spray, the baby bear would have lost its mother that day.

CD-4320 Survivors: High-Interest Nonfiction

Bear-Be-Gone!

Have you ever heard of mace? It's a pepper spray police officers use to **restrain** criminals. When sprayed in the face, attackers are in too much pain to fight back. Now, there is a spray just for bears. It helped a group of friends survive a bear attack.

Pat Goodwin and four of his friends went camping on Kodiak Island in Alaska. They knew the island had bears but chose not to take any guns. His friend Todd had purchased a can of pepper spray for bears. Goodwin and his friends laughed. They told Todd that he had wasted his money. As it turned out, the can of pepper spray saved their lives.

On the last day of their camping trip, they were heading down a trail and saw a bear. Then, they saw its baby. Pat quickly took out his camera to get a picture. Then, the mother bear, called a sow, began charging up the trail toward the hikers. They ran until they were cornered.

The sow wanted to protect her baby. She approached the frightened group slowly, growling and snorting.

When the bear was 15 feet away, Pat tried to light a flare to throw at her, but it didn't work. Then, Todd sprayed the sow with his mace. The bear pawed at her head, sneezing, and snorting. Then, she ran off. The pepper spray helped Pat, Todd, and their friends survive. It also saved the bear. If they had brought a gun instead of spray, the baby bear would have lost its mother that day.

Bear-Be-Gone!

Name: _____

1. What was the main idea of the last paragraph?
    A. Goodwin tried to throw a flare at the bear.
    B. Pepper spray for bears saved their lives.
    C. The bear began sneezing.
    D. The bear didn't like the pepper spray.

2. Answer the following questions.

    Where were Goodwin and his friends camping?

    _____

    What did they take for protection from bears?

    _____

    What did Goodwin think of the pepper spray before the attack?

    _____

    What did the bear do when she was sprayed?

    _____

3. Number the following events in the order they happened.
    _____ Goodwin tried to light a flare.

    _____ Goodwin and his friends went camping.

    _____ Goodwin got out his camera to take a picture.

    _____ On the last day of their trip they saw a bear.

    _____ The bear was sprayed with pepper spray.

4. What does the word **restrain** mean in the story?
    A. strain again
    B. hurt
    C. hold back
    D. trick

5. Why do you think Goodwin and his friends laughed at Todd and his pepper spray?
    A. Bears like pepper.
    B. Pepper spray for bears is expensive.
    C. They thought he was joking.
    D. They thought the pepper spray wouldn't work.

Bonus:
Write a story about a time when you had success when you didn't expect it.

97

A Caring Man

One hundred fifty years ago, there were no laws to protect animals and pets from abuse. Animals were thought of as private property that people could treat as they pleased. Horses were overworked, beaten, and not given water when they needed it. Hungry dogs and cats roamed the streets in search of food.

But that all started to change thanks to one man. Henry Bergh was a wealthy man from New York. In the early 1860s, he worked for the United States government in St. Petersburg, Russia. One day he saw a man beating a tired horse. He stopped his carriage, got out, and took the whip away from the astonished man. It was at that point that Bergh knew what he wanted to do with the rest of his life. He would work to protect animals from **cruel** people.

Bergh returned to New York and started the American Society for the Prevention of Cruelty to Animals (ASPCA) in 1866. He helped pass laws making cruelty to animals a crime.

Bergh walked the streets looking for injustice. If he saw a wagon too heavy for a horse to pull, he blocked the way until the load was lightened. He stopped the drowning of stray dogs and cats. He had drinking fountains for animals put on busy streets for horses pulling carts. He also made sure that circus animals were safe from fires by having their cages mounted on wheels. If he couldn't find a police officer to make an arrest, he arrested the person himself.

Many people made fun of him. They even called him "The Great Meddler," but he didn't care. He knew he was doing the right thing. Bergh would be proud to know that his work and dream survive today.

A Caring Man

One hundred fifty years ago, there were no laws to protect animals and pets from abuse. People thought they could treat animals as they pleased. Horses were over-worked. They were beaten and not given water when they needed it. Hungry dogs and cats looked for food in the streets.

But that all started to change thanks to one man. Henry Bergh was a rich man from New York. In the early 1860s, he worked for the United States government in Russia. One day, he saw a man beating a tired horse. He made the man stop. Bergh then knew what he would do with the rest of his life. He would protect animals from **cruel** people.

Bergh returned to New York. In 1866, he started the American Society for the Prevention of Cruelty to Animals (ASPCA). Then, he helped pass laws making cruelty to animals a crime.

Bergh walked the streets looking for abused animals. He made sure wagons were light enough for horses to pull. He stopped the drowning of stray dogs and cats. He had water fountains for horses put on busy streets. He also made sure that circus animals were safe from fires by having their cages mounted on wheels. He even arrested people himself.

Many people made fun of him. They even called him "The Great Meddler." Bergh didn't care. He knew he was doing the right thing. Bergh would be proud to know that his work and dream survive today.

99

A Caring Man

1. Choose another title for this story.
   A. Growing Up
   B. Cats and Dogs
   C. Horsing Around
   D. The Great Meddler

2. Answer the following questions.

   What do the letters ASPCA stand for?

   _____

   When was the ASPCA founded?

   _____

   Where was Henry Bergh from?

   _____

   When did Henry Bergh know what he
   wanted to do with the rest of his life?

   _____

3. Number the following events in the order
   they happened.

   _____ Bergh worked for the U.S. government.

   _____ Bergh helped pass laws making it
   illegal to mistreat animals.
   _____ Bergh founded the ASPCA.

   _____ Bergh stopped a man from beating
   his horse.
   _____ Bergh was called a meddler.

4. What does the word **cruel** mean in the
   story?
   A. mean
   B. gentle
   C. strange
   D. silly

5. Why do you think Henry Bergh was called
   "The Great Meddler"?
   A. Henry loved all animals no matter what
   their size or breeding.
   B. He could work with all kinds of metals.
   C. Some people thought how they treated
   their animals was none of Henry's business.
   D. People didn't like the fact that Henry
   was rich.

Bonus:

What is the biggest problem facing animals
and pets today? Research and write about how
the ASPCA is trying to help solve this problem.

A Dinosaur Named Sue

What weighs 7 tons, stands 13 feet tall, and is 67 million years old? Sue the Dinosaur. Sue, a Tyrannosaurus rex skeleton, was discovered in the summer of 1990. A fossil hunter named Sue Hendrickson uncovered it.

Hendrickson was working with her fossil collecting team at a dig site near the Black Hills in Faith, South Dakota. While the rest of her team went into town to fix a flat tire, Hendrickson stayed to look for fossils. Hendrickson spotted some bone fragments on the ground. Then, she found more bones in a nearby cliff. She climbed up the cliff for a better look and there it was. The biggest Tyrannosaurus rex ever found. Her teamed named the dinosaur "Sue" in her honor.

Sue wasn't the first T. rex skeleton found, but she is the largest, most complete, and best **preserved**. The first was found in 1900, but since then, only seven more have been unearthed that were more than half complete. Sue was ninety percent complete. Over two hundred of her bones were recovered.

Most of Sue's bones are in almost perfect condition. You can still see tiny lines that show where the muscles, tendons, and other soft tissues were attached to the bone. It took about three weeks to remove Sue from the rocky cliff. Then, it took years to clean the bones at a museum. Scientists can learn a lot about dinosaurs from Sue's remains, but one thing they may never know is whether Sue the T. Rex was a male or female.

Sue is on permanent display at The Field Museum in Chicago, Illinois. Two replicas of the skeleton are traveling around the United States. Maybe you'll see Sue at a museum near you!

A Dinosaur Named Sue

What weighs 7 tons, stands 13 feet tall, and is 67 million years old? Sue the Dinosaur. Sue's skeleton was found in the summer of 1990. It was a Tyrannosaurus rex. A fossil hunter named Sue Hendrickson found it.

Hendrickson and her team were digging near the Black Hills in Faith, South Dakota. Her team went into town to fix a flat tire. Hendrickson decided to stay to look for fossils. She saw some bone pieces on the ground. Then, she found more bones in a nearby cliff. She climbed up the cliff for a better look. There she saw the biggest Tyrannosaurus rex ever found. Her teamed named the dinosaur "Sue" in her honor.

The first T. rex skeleton was found in 1900. Since then, only seven more have been unearthed that were more than half complete. Sue is the largest, most complete, and best **preserved** T. rex ever found. They dug up over two hundred of her bones.

It took about three weeks to remove Sue from the cliff. Then, it took years to clean the bones at a museum. Scientists can learn a lot about dinosaurs from Sue. The one thing they may never know is whether Sue was really a male or female.

Sue is now on display at the Field Museum in Chicago, Illinois. Two copies of the skeleton are traveling around the United States. Maybe you'll see Sue at a museum near you!

CD-4320 Survivors: High-Interest Nonfiction

A Dinosaur Named Sue

Name: _____

1. What is the main idea of the second paragraph?
   A. Hendrickson found bone pieces on the ground.
   B. The fossil team went into town.
   C. The dinosaur was named after Hendrickson.
   D. Hendrickson found a large Tyrannosaurus rex.

2. Answer the following questions.

   How tall was Sue the T. Rex?

   _____

   How long did it take to remove Sue from the cliff?

   _____

   About how many of Sue's bones did they find?

   _____

   Why wasn't Hendrickson's team there when she found Sue?

   _____

3. Number the following events in the order they happened.

   _____ Sue the T. Rex walked the earth.

   _____ Scientists spent years cleaning Sue's bones.

   _____ Hendrickson saw some bone pieces on the ground.

   _____ Sue is on display at the Field Museum.

   _____ Sue was removed from the cliff.

4. What does the word **preserved** mean in the story?
   A. shaped
   B. turned into stone
   C. kept unbroken
   D. hardened

5. Why were two copies made of Sue's skeleton?
   A. They were made in case the original Sue was stolen.
   B. They were made so people didn't have to go to Chicago to see what Sue looks like.
   C. They were made to confuse people.
   D. They were made because scientists were afraid that the original Sue might fall apart.

Bonus:
Have you ever found something that had been lost for a very long time? Write about what it was and how you felt when you found it.

Here to Stay

Not many people like insects. They especially don't like cockroaches. But you have to **admire** them or at least give them credit. They have been around for millions of years. They were here on Earth before the dinosaurs and survived all kinds of weather, disasters, and predators.

You may have only seen one kind of cockroach, but there are over 4,000 species in the world. Cockroaches are arthropods that breathe through openings called "spiracles" in their lower bodies. One kind of cockroach, the Madagascar Hissing Cockroach, even makes a hissing sound when it breathes.

Cockroaches have survived because they adapt to their surroundings. They can also live a week without water and a month without food. You could even cut off a cockroach's head and the body could live for a week.

Cockroaches eat almost anything. They can eat camera film, books, and even clothing. They can survive for a month eating only the glue off of a postage stamp. They have teeth for grinding in their stomachs. After digestion, they excrete waste through 60 separate tubes.

Cockroaches have very sharp senses. A cockroach's hearing is much better than a human's. Cockroaches have two sensitive hairs around their bottoms. These hairs, called "cerci," respond to vibrations, including sound. Their eyes have 2,000 lenses that allow them to see in all directions. Humans only have one lens per eye.

Many bug sprays don't bother them. High levels of radiation don't even affect them. You may not like them, but they are here to stay.

Here to Stay

Cockroaches eat almost anything. They can eat camera film, books, and even clothing. They can live for a month eating only the glue off of a stamp. In their stomachs, they have teeth for grinding food.

Cockroaches have very sharp senses. A cockroach's hearing is much better than ours. Cockroaches have two sensitive hairs around their bottoms. These hairs are called "cerci." They feel movements and sound. Their eyes are better than ours are, too. They can see in all directions.

Many bug sprays and poisons don't bother them. You may not like them, but they are here to stay.

Not many people like insects. Most really don't like cockroaches. They call them pests. But you have to **admire** them. They have been around for millions of years. They were here before dinosaurs. They have survived all kinds of things.

There are over 4,000 different kinds of cockroaches in the world. Cockroaches are arthropods. They breathe through openings in their lower bodies. One kind of cockroach, the Madagascar Hissing Cockroach, even makes a hissing sound when it breathes.

Cockroaches have survived because they can live almost anywhere. They can also live a week without water and a month without food. If you cut off a cockroach's head, the body could live for a week.

Here to Stay

1. This story is about:
   A. the way cockroaches eat.
   B. how much fun cockroaches are.
   C. how cockroaches have managed to survive.
   D. what cockroaches look like.

2. Answer the following questions.

   How many different kinds of cockroaches are there?

   _____

   What do cockroaches eat?

   _____

   How long can a cockroach go without water?

   _____

   What do "cerci" help cockroaches to do?

   _____

3. Number the following facts in the order you learned about them in the story.

   _____ Cockroaches have teeth in their stomachs.
   _____ Cockroaches lived before the dinosaurs.
   _____ Cockroaches have a very good sense of hearing.
   _____ A cockroach can live a week without its head.
   _____ Most bug sprays don't bother them.

4. What does the word **admire** mean in the story?
   A. respect
   B. dislike
   C. love
   D. fear

5. How might a cockroach's sharp senses have helped it survive for so long?
   A. A cockroach's senses tell it if the weather is bad.
   B. A cockroach's senses warn it when danger is near.
   C. A cockroach's senses help it stay warm.
   D. A cockroach's senses help it see better than humans can.

Bonus:

Write a speech that would convince a parent to let their child have a cockroach for a pet.

106

Kiwi to the Rescue

Lisa Grey lives in Ontario, Canada with her family. She uses a wheelchair to get around. Another member of Lisa's family helps her every day. She is a dog named Kiwi. When Kiwi was a puppy, she was trained to help people. This training helped her save her owner's life.

One cold morning, after Lisa's family had gone shopping, Lisa was leaving their house to check their horses. As she steered her wheelchair onto the ramp out of the house, something went wrong. The wheelchair slipped, and she fell off the side of the ramp. The one hundred fifty-pound wheelchair fell on top of her. Lisa knew she was hurt badly and gave Kiwi the **command** to bring the phone.

Kiwi sprinted into action. First, Kiwi tried to bring a phone attached to a cord. The cord wasn't long enough. By the time Kiwi found a portable phone, Lisa was unconscious. Kiwi worked with the phone until she hit the redial button. The person on the other end heard only barking and knew there was trouble. An ambulance was sent to Lisa's address.

When the ambulance arrived at the Grey residence, they found Lisa under the wheelchair. Kiwi was lying across the part of Lisa that wasn't under the wheelchair. Kiwi knew her owner could not survive the sub-zero temperatures for long.

The ambulance workers had to lift Kiwi off her owner. When they put Lisa on the stretcher Kiwi jumped into the back of the ambulance. When the nurses at the hospital wondered what to do with Kiwi, the ambulance workers said to leave her with Lisa. Kiwi's quick actions helped her owner survive.

107

Kiwi to the Rescue

Lisa Grey lives in Ontario, Canada with her family. She uses a wheelchair to get around. She also has a dog named Kiwi. Kiwi was trained to help people. This training helped her save Lisa's life.

One cold morning, Lisa's family went shopping. Lisa was by herself. She left the house to check on their horses. As she moved her wheelchair out of the house, something went wrong. The wheelchair slipped. Lisa fell off the side of the ramp. The heavy wheelchair fell on top of her. Lisa knew she was hurt badly. She gave Kiwi the **command** to bring the phone.

Kiwi raced into action. First, Kiwi tried to bring a phone attached to a cord. The cord wasn't long enough. Kiwi found a portable phone, but by then Lisa had passed out. Kiwi worked with the phone until she hit the redial button. The person on the other end heard only barking. They knew there was trouble. An ambulance was sent to Lisa's address.

When the ambulance arrived, they found Lisa. The wheelchair was on top of her. Kiwi was also lying across the Lisa. Kiwi knew her owner could not survive the cold for long. So she kept her warm.

The ambulance workers had to lift Kiwi off her owner. When they put Lisa in the ambulance, Kiwi jumped in, too. The nurses at the hospital wondered what to do with Kiwi. The ambulance workers said to leave her with Lisa. Kiwi's quick actions helped Lisa survive.

Kiwi to the Rescue

Name: _____

1. What was the main idea of the second paragraph?
   A. Lisa was going to check on the horses.
   B. Lisa steers her wheelchair out of her house.
   C. Lisa was by herself.
   D. Lisa had an accident and needed help.

2. Answer the following questions.

   Why did Kiwi lay on top of Lisa after the accident?

   _____

   Why was Lisa by herself on the day of the accident?

   _____

   How did Kiwi save Lisa?

   _____

   How did Kiwi know to get the phone after the accident?

   _____

3. Number the following events in the order they happened.

   _____ Lisa's family went shopping.

   _____ Kiwi jumped into the ambulance.

   _____ Lisa got Kiwi as an animal helper.

   _____ Kiwi was trained to help people.

   _____ Lisa's wheelchair slipped off the ramp.

4. What does the word **command** mean in the story?
   A. treat
   B. order
   C. permission
   D. scolding

5. Why do you think the ambulance workers let Kiwi come to the hospital?
   A. They were afraid Kiwi would freeze outside.
   B. They were afraid Kiwi would bite them if they made her get out of the ambulance.
   C. They knew Kiwi was a specially trained dog and was there to help Lisa.
   D. They knew Kiwi would run away without Lisa there.

Bonus:
Write about whether or not you think animals should be used to help people. Explain your answer.

The Miracle Vine

Isn't surviving always a good thing? In the case of one pesky vine, this isn't always true. In 1876, the Japanese brought a plant called "kudzu" to Philadelphia. People fell in love with it right away. It had beautiful big leaves, and its purple flowers smelled great. Nobody suspected how much damage this vine could do.

Southerners in the United States decided to plant it in their fields. In the 1920s, they learned that their cows could eat the vine and it would grow back quickly. Very quickly. It can grow 60 feet a year and as much as a foot a day. "Who needs hay, when we've got kudzu?" they thought.

During the 1930s and 1940s, the government paid workers and farmers to plant kudzu in their fields. Kudzu stops soil **erosion**. It prevents land from washing away. But it also grows everywhere, especially in the humid Southeast. You can see it covering telephone poles, hillsides, houses, and abandoned cars. It quickly spread into forests and along roadsides. It killed trees and plants by covering them and blocking sunlight.

In 1953, the government changed its mind. They wanted people to stop planting kudzu. It was getting out of control and damaging forests and land everywhere. People weren't calling it a "miracle vine" anymore.

Unfortunately, it's not easy to stop kudzu. It's a survivor. Plant poisons called herbicides don't work on it. Sometimes they even make it grow better. It's hard to pull it out of the ground because the roots grow so deep.

People in the Southeast have found other uses for kudzu, though. It can be made into baskets, paper, food, and food for goats and cows. People now know they may have to live with kudzu for many years to come.

The Miracle Vine

Isn't surviving always a good thing? In the case of one pesky vine, this isn't always true. In 1876, the Japanese brought a plant called "kudzu" to Philadelphia. People fell in love with it. It had beautiful big leaves. Its purple flowers smelled great, too. Nobody knew how much damage this vine could do.

Farmers in the southeastern United States planted it in their fields. Their cows could eat the vine. Then, it would grow back quickly. Very quickly. It can grow 60 feet a year. It can even grow as much as a foot a day. It seemed better than hay.

During the 1930s and 1940s, the government paid workers and farmers to plant kudzu in their fields. Kudzu stops soil **erosion**. It prevents land from washing away. But it also grows everywhere, especially in the humid Southeast. You can see it covering telephone poles, hills, houses, and old cars. It quickly spread into forests and along roadsides. It killed trees and plants. It covered them and blocked out the sunlight.

In 1953, the government changed its mind. They wanted people to stop planting kudzu. It was getting out of control. It was damaging forests and land. People weren't happy with it anymore.

But it's not easy to stop kudzu. It's a survivor. Plant poisons don't work on it. Sometimes they even make it grow better. Also, it's hard to pull it out of the ground because the roots grow so deep.

People have found other uses for kudzu, though. It can be made into baskets, paper, food, and food for goats and cows. People now know they may have to live with kudzu for many years to come.

　　　　　　　CD-4320 Survivors: High-Interest Nonfiction

The Miracle Vine

1. What is the main idea of the second paragraph?
   A. Farmers planted kudzu in the south-eastern United States.
   B. Kudzu grows quickly.
   C. Cows like to eat kudzu.
   D. Farmers liked kudzu because it grew back quickly after cows ate it.

2. Answer the following questions.

   How long can kudzu grow in a day?

   _____

   When was kudzu brought to the United States?

   _____

   What are some of the uses for kudzu?

   _____

   What effect can plant poisons sometimes have on kudzu?

   _____

3. Number the following events in the order they happened.

   _____ The government wanted farmers to stop planting kudzu.
   _____ The Japanese brought kudzu to Philadelphia.
   _____ Farmers thought kudzu was a great thing to plant.
   _____ Kudzu started to spread across the southeastern United States.
   _____ People began to find other uses for kudzu.

4. What does the word **erosion** mean in the story?
   A. wearing away
   B. digging up
   C. thickness
   D. spreading

5. Why do you think kudzu grows so well in the southeastern United States?
   A. Because kudzu came from Japan.
   B. Because farmers planted so much of it.
   C. Because the weather is sunny, warm, and humid.
   D. All of the above.

Bonus:

Write a paragraph about a time when you got something that you thought was great at first but then turned out not to be what you expected.

Nine Lives

D o you believe cats have nine lives? If you do, then there is a cat named Scarlett that doesn't have many left.

Scarlett was a **stray** cat surviving in an old, vacant building in New York. One day the building caught fire. Most animals try to escape a situation like that. But Scarlett had five kittens to protect. One by one, she carried her babies to safety away from the burning building. As the fire got bigger, Scarlett ignored the danger and kept working. By the time Scarlett saved the last one, her fur was badly burned and her eyes were swollen shut.

A kind firefighter found the five kittens and went looking for the mother. Even though Scarlett could not see him, she trusted his voice and let him pick her up. He put her in a box with her babies. She couldn't see her kittens, so she counted them by touching each one's nose.

They were rushed to the nearest animal hospital where it took almost three months for them to heal from the fire. After that, the veterinarian made sure they were all adopted into good homes.

Scarlett and her heroic deed were in all of the local newspapers. Hundreds of people wanted to adopt Scarlett. Today, Scarlett's calico fur has all grown back and her eyes are opened wide. She plays with crinkled tissue paper balls, paper bags, and string like other cats. Then, she rests on the windowsill. She doesn't walk around like she's famous. She is just happy to live in a safe home with loving owners. To prove it, she purrs very loudly when her owners are near. Scarlett is a true survivor.

113

Nine Lives

Do you believe cats have nine lives? If you do, then there is a cat named Scarlett that doesn't have many left.

Scarlett was a **stray** cat. She lived in an old, empty building in New York. One day the building caught fire. Most animals try to get away from fire. But Scarlett had five kittens to save. One by one, she carried her babies away from the burning building. As the fire got bigger, Scarlett ignored the danger. She kept working. By the time Scarlett saved the last one, her fur was badly burned. Even her eyes were swollen shut.

A kind firefighter found the five kittens. Then, he went looking for the mother. Scarlett trusted his voice and let him pick her up. He put her in a box with her babies. She couldn't see her kittens, so she counted them by touching each one's nose.

They were rushed to the nearest animal hospital. It took almost three months for them to heal from the fire. After that, they made sure the cats were all adopted into good homes.

Scarlett's story was in all of the local newspapers. Hundreds of people wanted to adopt Scarlett. Today, Scarlett's calico fur has all grown back. Her eyes are opened wide. She plays with crinkled tissue paper balls, paper bags, and string like other cats. Then, she rests on the windowsill. She doesn't walk around like she's famous. She's just happy to live in a safe home with loving owners. To prove it, she purrs very loudly when her owners are near. Scarlett is a true survivor.

Nine Lives

1. Choose another title for this story.
   A. Too Many Cats
   B. Firefighter Hero
   C. Cat's Meow
   D. Mother's Love

2. Answer the following questions.

   In what state did this story take place?

   _____

   How many kittens did Scarlett have?

   _____

   How long did it take Scarlett and her kittens to heal?

   _____

   Where does Scarlett like to rest now?

   _____

3. Number the following events in the order they happened.

   _____ Scarlett was adopted.

   _____ The kittens were taken to the animal hospital.

   _____ An empty building caught on fire.

   _____ Scarlett carried out each kitten.

   _____ A firefighter found the kittens.

4. What does the word **stray** mean in the story?
   A. homeless
   B. wild
   C. tame
   D. dangerous

5. Why do you think the mother cat let the firefighter pick her up?
   A. She couldn't see and probably couldn't hear either.
   B. She was too hungry to run away.
   C. She decided she needed to trust someone.
   D. She heard her babies crying.

Bonus:
Animals know to run from danger. Write a paragraph about why you think Scarlett ignored her natural instincts and continued to go into the burning building.

Shark!

If anyone knew about the dangers of shark attacks and how to avoid them, it would be a professional lifeguard on the Florida coast. That's what Dawn Schauman thought, too. She had been a full-time lifeguard for six years, but she had never seen anyone badly hurt by a shark. That would soon change. One day in October 1993, Dawn went to work as usual. She knew it was the time of year when mullet fish swim close to the shore. Mullet fish, also called bait fish, attract sharks, but Dawn wasn't too worried about it.

At the time, Dawn was six and a half months pregnant and a nice swim in the ocean helped to relax her and keep her in shape. Before lunch she told her partner she was going for a swim. Since it was fall, there was only an elderly couple on the beach, so it seemed like a good time to take a break.

Dawn swam out about seventy-five yards and began her water exercises. The next thing she knew, something smashed into her left side and spun her completely around. Like anyone under these circumstances, her first reaction was to **panic**. But she realized that would be the worst thing she could do. With a burning pain in her arm and leg she swam toward the shore. Her thigh had been torn badly, and she was bleeding. She knew a shark had bitten her.

When Dawn finally made it to safety, she found her partner who immediately called for a rescue unit. Dawn was in pain but was more concerned about her baby. She was rushed to the hospital. The doctors were able to save her arm, leg, and baby boy. He was born two and a half months later and was named Macintyre William Shark Schauman.

116

Shark!

Dawn Schauman had been a full-time lifeguard for six years. She had never seen anyone badly hurt by a shark. That would soon change. One day in October 1993, Dawn went to work as usual. She knew it was the time of year when mullet fish swim close to the shore. Mullet fish, also called bait fish, attract sharks. Still, Dawn wasn't too worried.

At the time, Dawn was six and a half months pregnant. She thought a nice swim in the ocean would help her relax. There was only an elderly couple on the beach. It seemed like a good time to take a break. She told her partner where she was going.

Dawn swam out about seventy-five yards. Then, she began her water exercises. The next thing she knew, something smashed into her left side. It spun her completely around. She started to **panic**, but then she stopped. She knew that would be the worst thing she could do. So with a burning pain in her arm and leg, she swam toward the shore. Her thigh had been torn badly, and she was bleeding. She knew a shark had bitten her.

Dawn finally made it to safety. She found her partner who called for help. Dawn was in pain, but she was more worried about her baby. She was rushed to the hospital. The doctors were able to save her arm, leg, and baby boy. He was born two and a half months later. He was named Macintyre William Shark Schauman.

117

Shark!

1. What is the main idea of the third paragraph?
   A. A shark attacked Dawn as she was swimming in the ocean.
   B. Swimming helped Dawn relax.
   C. A shark slammed into Dawn's left side.
   D. Dawn was bleeding when she swam toward shore.

2. Answer the following questions.

   Where did the shark bite Dawn?

   _____

   What warning sign didn't worry Dawn when she went for a swim?

   _____

   How long had Dawn been a life guard?

   _____

   What was Dawn most worried about after she made it to safety?

   _____

3. Number the following events in the order they happened.

   _____ Dawn told her partner she was going for a swim.
   _____ Dawn was rushed to the hospital.

   _____ A shark bit Dawn while she was swimming.
   _____ Macintyre William Shark Schauman was born.
   _____ Dawn became a lifeguard.

4. What does the word **panic** mean in the story?
   A. swim wildly
   B. lose control
   C. scream
   D. cry for help

5. Why was it a good time for Dawn to swim when there was only an elderly couple on the beach?
   A. They wouldn't bother her.
   B. She could take a break without having to worry about saving anyone.
   C. The water was probably warm.
   D. They would save her if she was attacked by a shark.

Bonus:
Why do some sharks attack people? Research and write about what you learn.

Surviving Giants

Did you know that there are giants living in the mountains of California? They drink water and make their own food. But there is no need to fear these gentle giants known as giant sequoias (sa-koy-yas).

Giant sequoias are the biggest trees in the world. They're also the largest living things on Earth. They can grow as tall as 300 feet high and live several thousand years. These **enormous** trees survive because they grow quickly. A sapling, or baby giant sequoia, can grow two feet per year. Once a giant sequoia reaches 200-300 feet, it begins growing outward instead of upward. Some of oldest trees are 35-feet wide!

The beginning of life for the giant sequoia isn't easy. It starts life as a small cone on a large tree. A special squirrel, called a Douglas Squirrel, eats the cone and drops the seeds on the forest floor. If conditions are right, a seed will begin to grow into a sapling. The sapling must survive bad weather and animals that eat young trees, such as deer. If the tree survives for several hundred years, it will reach its full height. Then, the giant sequoia begins producing cones and the process begins again.

The giant sequoia has few natural enemies. It is now against the law to cut down a giant sequoia. The only place they grow naturally is in California. Now, most of them die from falling over. In the past, there were many giant sequoias. The last ice age killed most of them.

People are working hard to preserve the giant sequoias. Sequoias have been planted in a few places around the world. But people must continue protecting them. If they don't, giant sequoias might not survive.

CD-4320 Survivors: High-Interest Nonfiction

Surviving Giants

Did you know that giants live in California? They drink water and make their own food. They're called giant sequoias (sa-koy-yas).

Giant sequoias are the biggest trees in the world. They're also the largest living things on Earth. They can grow as tall as 300 feet high and live several thousand years. These **enormous** trees survive because they grow fast. A sapling, or baby tree, can grow two feet per year. Once a giant sequoia reaches 200-300 feet, it begins growing outward instead of upward. Some of oldest trees are 35-feet wide!

A giant sequoia starts life as a small cone on a large tree. A special squirrel, called a Douglas Squirrel, eats the cone. Then, it drops the seeds on the forest floor. A seed will begin to grow into a sapling. The sapling must survive bad weather and animals that eat young trees, such as deer. When it reaches full height, the giant sequoia starts making cones. More baby trees will be on the way.

It is now against the law to cut down a giant sequoia. The only place they grow naturally is California. Now, most of them die from falling over. Once, there were many giant sequoias. The last ice age killed most of them.

People are working hard to save the giant sequoias. Sequoias have been planted in a few places around the world. But people must protect these trees. If they don't, giant sequoias might not survive.

Surviving Giants

Name: _____

1. What was the main idea of the third paragraph?
   A. Deer like to eat young giant sequoias.
   B. The life of a giant sequoia has many diffi-cult steps.
   C. Once a giant sequoia grows to a certain height, it has an easy life.
   D. Baby giant sequoias rarely survive.

2. Answer the following questions.

   How fast do baby giant sequoias grow?

   _____

   How tall can a giant sequoia grow?

   _____

   Where do giant sequoias live today?

   _____

   What killed many of the giant sequoias?

   _____

3. Number the following events in the order they happened.

   _____ A squirrel eats the cone.

   _____ The sapling starts to grow outward.

   _____ The squirrel drops the seeds.

   _____ The sapling grows to full height.

   _____ The seed begins to grow.

4. What does the word **enormous** mean in the story?
   A. huge
   B. insignificant
   C. hearty
   D. short

5. Why do you think it's against the law to cut down giant sequoias?
   A. There are so few giant sequoias left that we need to protect them.
   B. If we cut them all down, they will be extinct.
   C. If we cut them all down, there wouldn't be any more cones.
   D. All of the above.

Bonus:
Write a paragraph telling what you think should be done to protect the giant sequoias.

Woolly Survivor

Finding the remains of **extinct** animals is not new. It happens often, but it is always exciting. Scientists are very happy when they find several bones, teeth, or horns of the same animal in one place. When they find more than half the bones of an animal, that's big news. To find hair, scales, skin or anything like that is extremely rare. To find a whole animal in frozen mud along with the plants and insects that lived at that time would be completely out of the question. Or would it?

Woolly Mammoths first appeared about 120,000 years ago. They liked cold areas and were part of the elephant family. Woolly mammoths were the size of modern Asian elephants. These huge animals had a shaggy covering of long, thick hair. They also had long curved tusks that they used like snowplows to uncover food.

A whole, frozen woolly mammoth was found in Siberia in 1999. Its remains had survived in ice for over 20,000 years! Scientists from all over the world were excited. They decided to cut out the giant block of ice. Then, they used a helicopter to move it to an ice cave where scientists used hair dryers to slowly melt away the ice. It took a long time because they wanted to be very careful.

Some scientists are more excited about the other things found in the ice. They believe that by studying the plants and insects they may learn why woolly mammoths became extinct. Other scientists are hoping for good blood samples. They want to try to clone, or make more, baby woolly mammoths.

Scientists are hoping to learn many things from this one remarkable mammoth.